SAINTS OF
NORTHUMBRIA

SAINTS OF NORTHUMBRIA

EDITED AND PRESENTED
BY IAIN MACDONALD

FLORIS BOOKS

First published in English in 1997 by Floris Books

British Library CIP Data available

ISBN 0-86315-252-X

Printed in Great Britain
by Page Bros, Norwich

Contents

Contents

Introduction

The Northumbria which produced so many remarkable saints in the seventh century was a kingdom much larger than the Northumbria of today.
Although its borders were by no mean always well
defined, it comprised at its greatest extent our
counties of the Lothians, Berwick, Roxburgh,
Selkirk, Northumberland, Cumberland, Westmor-
land, Durham and York, with incursions into
Lancashire and even Cheshire. To the north across
the Forth was the kingdom of the Picts. To the
west lay the British kingdom of Strathclyde and to
the south the Angle kingdoms of Mercia and
Lindsey.

Northumbria in the seventh century was the
scene of the surge and ebb of many tides and
streams of human life and endeavour. In that
region Angle and Briton, Pict and Gael met, sometimes in conflict, sometimes harmoniously inter-
mingling. There was the confluence of the worship
of Celtic deities, of Germanic gods, the older
Christianity of the Britons, the Christianity sweep-
ing northward from Rome and the Celtic Christianity flowing eastward from Iona and Ireland.

These streams, too, were at times peacefully joined and at times in bitter dispute.

Of these times, history has forgotten much, as events for the most part went unrecorded. Indeed, for a great deal of our knowledge of that era we are indebted to one man, the Venerable Bede.

Scanty though the historical records are, it is possible to follow the broad lines of the story leading up to this confluence of race and religion, a brief outline of which now follows.

The Britons

The Britons were indigenous to Northumbria from prehistoric times. During the Roman occupation of Britain, it would appear that all the tribes south of Hadrian's Wall were Britons, as well as those beyond Hadrian's Wall to the north as far as the Forth and Clyde. The Romans named the tribe in South-East Scotland the Votadini, their neighbours to the west the Selgovae, in Galloway the Novantae, and a great tribe occupying the north of England, the Brigantes.

Roman historians were more concerned with identifying tribes than peoples of the same language, for the Romans showed little interest in contemporary foreign tongues and left us no description of them. Modern historians conclude that the people of Northumbria undoubtedly spoke a language of which Welsh is the descendant.

After the departure of the Romans from Britain in 410, the history and wars of the British tribes fade into sparsely recorded time. However, by the dawn of the seventh century we find British kingdoms in Strathclyde, Cumbria and Gwynedd.

The Picts

The Picts are a mysterious people and a puzzle to the historians. No trace of their language remains; no Pictish chronicles were written. Some historians believe them to be related in language to the Britons, others to the Gaels, and others that they were a pre-Celtic people. They are mentioned by Roman historians as the Picti, or painted people, or — it is also suggested — *Pictus* was simply the Latin form of the original name of the people. They appear in Irish annals and at last in Bede's *Historia Ecclesiastica*. Their own memorial lives on in their wonderful stone carvings. In Roman times they were probably the original Caledonians who gave the Romans so much trouble and were never subjected to them. By the beginning of the seventh century their kingdoms stretched from Orkney to the Forth-Clyde line. At some time after the departure of the Romans the Picts had also established a powerful presence and dominion in the

British kingdom of the Lothians and south-east Scotland.

The Gaels

Ireland was the home of the Gaels from prehistoric times. About the year 500 AD, Gaels crossed over from Ireland and established themselves in what is now Argyll (Earra-Gaidheal). By the beginning of the seventh century they formed the strong kingdom of Dalriada. Both the Gaels who remained in Ireland and those of Dalriada bear the name *Scotti* in Bede's history, and no distinction is made between them. The appellation *Scotus* then generally denotes someone who is Irish.

The Angles

The original home of the Angles was a district on the Baltic coast of Schleswig, formerly called Angel, lying between Flensburg and Rendsburg. They were of the same speech and race as the Saxons. Their westward adventures began later than those of the Saxons but by the middle of the sixth century they had obtained footholds in the river valleys of eastern England north of the Stour in Essex. By the beginning of the seventh century the Angles had founded the kingdoms of Bernicia, Deira, Mercia and East Anglia in the North, East and Midlands of England while Saxons and Jutes had founded kingdoms to the south.

It is remarkable that it is the Angles who have given the name to all England and the English, but it is the Saxons who have left their name in Gaelic, Welsh and Breton, in which languages the English are referred to as Saxons.

Pre-Christian religions in Britain

The Romans who, as already mentioned, were notoriously uninterested in the grammar and languages of the peoples whom they conquered, were nonetheless very interested in the religions and cults of those peoples. From their accounts, and from the myths written down in later centuries by Irish, Icelandic and other writers, we know something of the gods of the four pagan peoples already mentioned.

In the main, these deities were folk-deities rather than universal deities, and their cults and worship were local and diverse. The Romans were keen to absorb and propitiate the gods of the peoples whom they had overcome. They therefore tried to find out as much as possible about the worship of those tribes, and indeed to equate those gods with their own.

Between the peoples of different pagan religions there does not appear to have been any missionary work, any attempt to convert from one religion to another. Thus it was possible for different religions and cults to exist alongside.

At the beginning of the seventh century, the pagan religions of Britons, Picts, Gaels and Angles were still very much alive, with Christianity in its various forms flowing and ebbing around them. But the few monk-scribes of the seventh century give us no picture of the nature of pagan religion at that time. For them all pagans worshipped either nameless idols or devils.

Early British and Celtic Christianity

Legend surrounds the first coming of Christianity to Britain, and history does not tell of the source of Christianity in Ireland before St Patrick.

History does tell us however that Christianity was widespread in Britain by the end of the Roman occupation (410).

We know that Pelagius, a British or Irish Christian, went with reforming zeal to Rome about 400, that St Ninian *(c.* 360–431) a Cumbrian Briton was brought up as a Christian before he also went to Rome to receive his mission to his fellow-countrymen of Cumbria, that St Germanus (429) rallied the Christian Britons against the Picts and Saxons, that St Patrick was a British Christian before he too went to Rome and was consecrated.

Legend and mystery, too, enshroud the true origins of the Celtic Church in Ireland, for there are historical indications that Christianity was known there before the coming of St Patrick.

At all events between the death of St Patrick (492) and the departure of St Columba for Iona in 563, the Celtic Church was well established in Ireland.

During the fifth and sixth centuries the story of the spread of Christianity among the Britons in the south of Scotland and in Northumbria sinks into historical oblivion. In Culross about the year 520 we find St Severus (Serf or Servanus), the foster-father of St Kentigern, but was he Irish, Pictish or British, and where did he get his Christianity from? Later in Melrose we find St Boswell (Boisil), but little else is known of the work of missionary monks and whence they came.

In short at the beginning of the seventh century we see a Christian presence in Pictland, Dalriada, Strathclyde in Scotland and a Christian presence in Gwynedd and the British regions of England and Wales, and a thoroughly pagan culture among the Angles.

The Emergence of the Roman Church

The story of the collapse of the Roman Empire in the West and the emergence of the Church of Rome as the Roman Catholic Church with the Pope at its head is long and complex. Before however the curtain opens on the whole drama, three momentous actions took place.

The most significant of these was the decision of the Emperor Constantine (306–337) to make Christianity the official religion of the Roman empire (in 324). Having adopted Christianity as the state-religion, though not yet baptized himself, he went further: it was his aim that there should be unity of practice and belief among the Christians, for at that time there were many groups — Nestorians, Copts, Manichaeans and notably Arians — all with different tenets and philosophies. Constantine himself called and presided over the famous Council of Nicaea (325) which gave to the Church the Nicene Creed and which condemned but did not destroy Arian Christianity. In this controversy the Bishop of Rome declared for the Nicene forms, laying the foundation for what was to become the Roman Catholic doctrine and rite.

Constantine's other great action was the founding of the city of Constantinople (310) and the transfer of his capital there from Rome. This left a power vacuum and weakness in Italy, a vacuum which was to be filled on the one hand by the incursion of the Germanic barbarian peoples, and on the other by the emergence of the Church of Rome as a religious and political centre in the West.

The third great influence was the work of the Arian Christian missionaries among the Germanic peoples along the Eastern-Northern borders of the empire. The most famous missionary was the Gothic Bishop Ulfila (310–380) who translated the Bible into Gothic. To Christianity were converted not only the Goths, but also many other Germanic peoples, notably the Lombards and Burgundians, who lived mostly beyond the limits of the Roman Empire but also at times as *foederati* within its territories.

Some seventy years after the transfer to Constantinople, seventy years of turbulence within the Empire and of wars upon its borders, the collapse of the western half of the Empire began.

In the year 406 Vandals, Alans and Suevi crossed the Rhine and broke into Gaul and after devastating the country moved south to the Pyrenees. They were followed by the Alemanni and Burgundians. From Illyria the Goths overran the Western Roman world and established kingdoms in Italy, Southern France and Spain. The Goths were soon followed by the Lombards. But because these peoples were already Christian they did not destroy

the Christian Church in those countries, but
venerated it. Though Alaric the Goth sacked
Rome (410) he revered the Bishop of Rome,
Innocent I. On the ashes of the Roman Empire,
Innocent claimed the primacy of the See of Rome
among the Christian Churches, and thus the first
step towards the supremacy of the Church of
Rome in the West was taken.

Goths, Lombards and Burgundians carved out
kingdoms and established themselves as barbarian
aristocrats among the civilized native Latin population of Italy and the Gallo-Roman population of
Southern France. Latin language and Roman
administration prevailed and the conquerors adap-
ted to Roman civilization. The Church thrived and
grew in strength. It set itself intermittently the task
of converting the Arian Goths, Lombards and
Burgundians to the Catholic faith; but Arianism
lingered on for another two centuries.

Neither the Ostrogothic, Visigothic nor Burgun-
dian kingdoms extended over the northern part of
France. Hardly had the Gallo-Romans recovered
from the onslaught of Vandals, Alans and Suevi in
406 and re-established themselves, when they were
overwhelmed by a fresh invasion. This time it was
the conquering Franks from Germany, a pagan
warrior people. Under their king, Clovis (481–
511), they, like their German cousins in the south
established themselves as a ruling aristocracy over

the native Gallo-Roman population. Though pagan they did not destroy the Church, but on the contrary saw its value in the administration of the kingdom and befriended it. In Northern Gaul then we have a native population, Christian and civilized, speaking Latin, and a pagan barbarian aristocracy and royalty speaking the Frankish form of the Germanic language, but this was not to last for soon the Franks adopted the language of their subjects.

In the Kingdom of Burgundy Catholicism was firmly established. Princess Clotilde (St Clotilde), daughter of King Chilperic, was a devout Christian. King Clovis of the Franks sought an alliance with Burgundy and a wife. In 493 Clotilde married the pagan king. Three years later he was baptized a Christian and three thousand Franks with him.

A hundred years later the King of the Franks was Charibert (561–567). He had a daughter Bertha (St Bertha). King Charibert gave his daughter in marriage *(c.* 580) to the pagan Aethelbert (560–616), king of the pagan Jutes of Kent. On her marriage Princess Bertha brought her Frankish father-confessor, Bishop Liudhard, with her. This opened the door to the mission of St Augustine to the Jutes of Kent (597). King Aethelbert accepted the Christian faith and was baptized by St Augustine, through whose work the Church of Rome gained a firm footing in the south-east of England. But while Augustine had won over the worshippers of Wotan, he came hard up against the British bishops of the Welsh Christian Church and succeeded in antagonizing them, perhaps a prelude to the controversy which later came to its head at the Synod of Whitby.

King Aethelbert and Queen Bertha had a son Eadbert and a daughter (later St) Aethelburga. Eadbert, although baptized, reverted to paganism when he ascended the throne of Kent (616), but later became a devout Christian. Aethelburga was brought up and remained a devout Christian of the Roman Church, and we shall see how through her the Roman Church came to Northumbria.

Wars of the kings of Bernicia and Deira

We have seen how by the end of the sixth century the Angles had established the pagan kingdoms of Bernicia, Deira, Mercia and East Anglia. These kingdoms did not present a common front against the other peoples of Britain but were often at enmity with each other and in alliance with British, Pictish and Irish (Gaelic) kings.

Our story here begins with King Aethelric of Bernicia (who reigned 586–593) and King Aella of Deira who were contemporaries. King Aethelric had a son, Aethelfrith the fierce. Aethelfrith's first wife was Bebba, but after her death he married Acha, King Aella's daughter which presaged the union of Bernicia and Deira. But the union did not come about through this marriage but in quite contrary fashion. When King Aella died (588) Aethelric marched into Deira and annexed it. After the death of Aethelric in 593 Aethelfrith inherited the combined kingdoms, now known as Northumbria. The reign of Aethelfrith the fierce (593–616) was full of wars and battles. He fought against Britons, Picts and Gaels, greatly extending his kingdom.

Acha's brother was Edwin, heir of Deira. He fled from Deira when Aethelric marched in, and spent many years in exile. His first refuge was among the Britons of Gwynedd. Thence he came to King Cearl of Mercia where he married Cearl's daughter Coenburh. No doubt the Mercian king had respect for the long arm of Aethelfrith seeking to destroy Edwin, for next we find Edwin with Raedwald, King of East Anglia. Raedwald proved a doughty champion to Edwin for he marched against Aethelfrith, defeated and slew him at the Battle of the River Idle (616).

Edwin was now King of Northumbria. In his turn he drove out Aethelfrith's family. Whether he was ever reconciled to his sister Acha and what-happened to her is not recorded. She and her husband Aethelfrith had three sons and a daughter.

The eldest son, Eanfrith escaped to Pictland where he married a Pictish princess and became a Christian. The next two sons, Oswald and Oswy escaped to Dalriada and Iona, taking their sister Ebba with them. These three were baptized into the Celtic Church while in exile. All four come back into the story after Edwin's death in 632.

Roman Christianity reaches Northumbria

The reign of King (later St) Edwin (616–632), like that of his forerunners, was filled with wars and conquests with the power of Northumbria ever waxing. At some point his pagan wife Coenburh died and he was free to marry again. This time (625) he sought the hand of Princess Aethelburga of Kent. Her brother, King Eadbert, stipulated that she should remain a Christian. Edwin, who, although pagan, was no stranger to Christianity which he had encountered during his exile, agreed. Accordingly Aethelburga came north with the newly consecrated bishop, St Paulinus, as her spiritual father, and married Edwin. Two years later Edwin with his two sons by his first marriage was baptized at York by Paulinus who was now established as Bishop of York. Edwin became a staunch supporter of the Church.

Christian or pagan, Edwin was like his brother-in-law Aethelfrith a great conqueror. He extended the Kingdom of Northumbria northward through the Lothians as far as Edwinburg, westward into Cumbria and Galloway and to the borders of Gwynedd in Wales and southward into Mercia. He also destroyed the British kingdom of Elmet (in West Yorkshire) and incorporated its lands into Northumbria.

One result of these campaigns was that the way was opened more easily for the Church of York to communicate with the Christian foundation of Whithorn (St Ninian's) in Galloway.

Another result was that Edwin made many enemies, chief of whom were Cadwalla, the British King of Gwynedd, a Christian, and Cadwalla's ally, Penda, King of Mercia, an Angle and a Pagan. In 632 Cadwalla and Penda attacked Edwin and killed him at the Battle of Hatfield Chase.

Edwin's eldest son, Osfrith, was killed in the same battle. Eadfrith, his second son was taken prisoner by Penda and later killed by him. Aethelburga and her children were now in peril. St Paulinus took the fugitive family back to Kent where they found refuge with King Eadbert. The family included Aethelburga's daughter Eanflaed who, as we shall see, returned later to Northumbria. Aethelburga herself, however, eventually took the veil and founded the monastery of Liming in Kent.

With the departure of St Paulinus a shadow fell

over the Christian Church in Northumbria, but the light was not completely extinguished for Paulinus had left his deacon, James, who maintained the Christian presence in York during the dark years which followed.

Between Paulinus and Aidan (632–634)

After the Battle of Hatfield Chase, Cadwalla made himself overlord of Northumbria but split the kingdom allowing the Bernicians to choose Eanfrith, Aethelfrith's eldest son as their king, and Osric, first cousin of King St Edwin to be King of Deira. Eanfrith accordingly came down from Pictland, but his reign did not last long as he was soon killed by Cadwalla. A similar fate overtook Osric for he too was killed in war against Cadwalla. Both Eanfrith and Osric had reverted to paganism which was clearly still very much alive.

But soon Aethelfrith's second son, Oswald, returning from exile appeared on the scene. With a small Christian army, perhaps composed of his friends the Gaels as well as Northumbrians, he defeated and killed Cadwalla at Hefenfelth (Heavenfield) in 634.

Oswald now became King of Northumbria. He immediately sent to Iona for monks to re-establish Christianity in Northumbria. The first missionary was not a success, but then Aidan came and the king established him as first Bishop of Lindisfarne.

The thirty years before the Synod of Whitby

King Oswald, now remembered as a saint and martyr, reigned for only seven years (634–641)★. On the one hand he actively assisted St Aidan in the latter's missionary work and on the other he was beset with much fighting which earned him great respect among the neighbouring kings. In the end Penda, the pagan king of Mercia, the old enemy of the Northumbrians, defeated and killed King Oswald at the battle of Maserfelth (Oswestry) in 641.

After the death of Oswald on the battlefield, the Kingdom of Northumbria once more fell apart. For their king the Bernicians chose Oswy, Oswald's brother, while the Deirans chose Oswin, son of that unfortunate King Osric who had been killed by Cadwalla.

Now Oswald had a son Aethelwald who curiously enough became friendly with his father's enemy Penda, but he was still a boy, so we shall leave him in the wings awaiting his cue to reappear on the scene.

★ Bede reckons nine years, adding two years of King Eanfrith's reign to Oswald's, because Eanfrith had renounced the Christian Faith. *(Hist. Ecc.* III.1.)

About the time when Oswy became King of Bernicia he was already a widower. By his first wife, Riemmelth he had two children; a son, Alchfrith and a daughter Alchflaed. These two we shall also leave in the wings until their turn comes to reappear on the scene.

Now King Oswy was free to marry and whom should he choose but his cousin Eanflaed, daughter of his old enemy and uncle, St Edwin who had driven him into exile. They were married in 643 and Eanflaed became Queen of Bernicia. She fostered the Church, both Celtic and Roman, but she herself followed the Roman practices while her husband followed the Celtic practices. These divergencies came to a head as we shall see some twenty years later.

King Oswy supported St Aidan in his work, and Aidan also worked in Deira where King Oswin also was his patron. Aidan died in 651 and was succeeded by St Finan as Bishop of Lindisfarne. It was in this year that Cuthbert entered the monastery of Melrose (Mailross, now Old Melrose). Melrose had been founded by monks of the Celtic Church. St Boisil (Boswell) was prior and St Eata, a Northumbrian, provost.

Events now took a startling turn. King Oswy marched into Deira (651) and drove out Oswin, whom he later caused to be killed. As sub-king of

Deira he allowed the Deirans to choose Aethel-wald, St Oswald's son. Aethelwald died some three years later and Oswy's own son Alchfrith succeeded him as sub-king. Alchfrith became a firm supporter of the Roman Church, but not yet in any opposition to the Celtic Church for he was friendly with St Finan.

Although Penda allowed his son Peada and his daughter Cyniburg to be baptized and to allow Peada to marry Oswy's daughter Alchflaed and to give his daughter Cyniburg as wife to Alchfrith, none of this stopped him from renewing the war against the Northumbrians. He marched against King Oswy but was defeated and killed at the battle of Winwaed (655). This ended the Mercian supremacy and Oswy was now the undisputed King of all Northumbria.

In 661 St Finan died and was succeeded by St Colman as bishop of Lindisfarne. St Boisil also died in that year and St Cuthbert was elected prior. Meantime the power and prestige of King Oswy increased so that he was recognized as overlord of all the kingdoms of England, and of parts of Pict-land and Strathclyde with the title of Bretwalda.

During these decades the Celtic Church had been very active with missions being sent to the neighbouring Angle kingdoms, while the Roman Church from Canterbury had been no less active.

There were differences between the two Churches, not so much in doctrine as in liturgy and practice, serious enough to cause dissention. In true kingly fashion King Oswy determined to resolve the issues by calling a council of both Churches at which also royalty and nobility were present. This council he convened in the year 664 at the Abbey of Streanaeshalch where St Hilda was Abbess. In later times Streanaeshalch* became known as Hviteby (White-town), whence Whitby, and the Council became known as the Synod of Whitby. The issues which came to the forefront were the manner of calculating when Easter should fall, and the form of tonsure. But one senses that the real tensions went far deeper.

Among all those present at the Synod we should mention the more important. First King Oswy who acted as President, Chairman and Judge giving the final verdict. Then his son King Alchfrith, a champion of the Roman party and patron of St Wilfrid, but whether he spoke or not is not recorded. Neither is it recorded whether the Queens Eanfled and Cyniburg were present, but it is certain that

* The meaning of the name *Streanaeshalch* has not been determined by modern scholars. Bede glosses it as *'Sinus Fari'* ('the bay of the lighthouse'). It is unlikely that Bede would translate an Old English name. I suggest therefore that *Streanaeshalch* derives from the Irish, for St Hilda who founded the abbey was an adherent of St Aidan. In modern Scots Gaelic, akin to Irish Gaelic, *Sron an t-Seallaidh* ('The Headland of the View(point)') sounds not unlike *Streanaeshalch,* and the abbey was built upon the headland, not in the bay. Could Bede have been misinformed about the meaning?

their influence and interest played a very important part.

There was the venerable Bishop Colman, spokesman for the Celtic Church. Facing him was Bishop Agilbert, a Frank by birth, who had studied in the south of Ireland in a monastery of the Roman Church. He was no master of the Anglian language (Old English) and requested one, Wilfrid, to speak for him. Now Wilfrid had been brought up in the Celtic Church, but had travelled widely in Gaul and Italy, had been to Rome and was a fervent convert to the Roman way. There was also the venerable Bishop Cedd who acted as interpreter. It is not recorded in what languages he interpreted or why an interpreter was needed. Did Colman speak only Gaelic? Or did all the ecclesiastics speak in Latin and Cedd translated into English? St Cedd was a Northumbrian, one of four brothers, all trained by St Aidan and who all became churchmen.

At the end of the Synod King Oswy declared in favour of the Roman practices.

After the Synod of Whitby

Colman could not accept King Oswy's decision to introduce the Roman practices into the bishopric of Lindisfarne, but because he was a friend of the King, he was able to depart in peace. He recommended Tuda to be his successor and the King appointed the latter Bishop of Lindisfarne. Then taking with him not only a party of Irish (Scottish) but also a party of English monks, Colman departed to Iona to confer with the fathers of the Celtic Church. Later he went to Ireland and founded a monastery at Innishboffin with Irish and English monks.

After the Synod of Whitby, Cedd returned to his monastery at Lastingham, where he died of the plague later in the same year of the Synod. His brother, St Chad, succeeded him there as abbot.

It was not only with Celtic churchmen that Wilfrid in his lifetime clashed. Indeed we could readily imagine Wilfrid as a warrior armed with a battle-axe for he was an inveterate fighter. He quarrelled with kings and queens, bishops and archbishops; but he did not quarrel with the Pope.

After the death of Bishop Tuda (later in 664) who succeeded Colman, the see of Lindisfarne was divided into three bishoprics: Lindisfarne, York and Ripon. Wilfrid was made Bishop of Ripon.

By then Canterbury, but not York, had become an archbishopric, and now we find the Archbishop of Canterbury, Theodore, appointing bishops all over the Saxon and Angle kingdoms whereas hitherto this had been done by the kings. In 669

Theodore appointed Wilfrid Bishop of York as well as of Ripon.

For the next few years Wilfrid's material star rose. He caused great minsters, churches and monasteries to be built, and he acquired great estates. During this time King Oswy died (670) and he was succeeded by his son Ecgfrith. At first all went well for Wilfrid but in the end he quarrelled with Ecgfrith who expelled him from Northumbria in 679.

The account of Wilfrid's lifelong quarrel with the kings of Northumbria and with Archbishop Theodore is a long story, involving Wilfrid in two journeys to the Pope in Rome and a period of missionary work among the South Saxons, and another period in Mercia.

Although Wilfrid had been brought up in the monastery at Lindisfarne under St Finan he went to Rome when he was eighteen and there became a staunch adherent of the Roman Church. His whole being is charged with the spirit of Rome: territorial organization, legal exactness, the search for strict orthodox doctrine, decisive suppression of heresy, the rights and powers of the ecclesiastical hierarchy. In all this Wilfrid had travelled spiritually very far from his alma mater, Lindisfarne, and the peaceful monks by the sea.

The early life of St Hilda

Not from Bede but from Florence of Worcester do we hear about the story of Hilda's childhood and youth. We go back to the time of King Aethelfrith of Bernicia (593–616) who marched into Deira and drove out his son-in-law St Edwin. Edwin had a nephew Hereric who also fled from Aethelfrith and sought refuge with King Cerdic, a Briton, whose Kingdom was Elmet (in West Yorkshire). Thither Hereric went with his wife Bregswid and there they had three daughters the third of whom was Hilda. Cerdic however was no friend of the Angles and not long after Hereric died of poison. When St Edwin became King of Northumbria after Aethelfrith's defeat at the battle of the River Idle (616), he took revenge on Cerdic, invaded his kingdom, drove him out and annexed Elmet to Northumbria. He brought Bregswid and her children back to Northumbria with him. The rest of the story is told by Bede.

The Churches after the Synod

Although at the Synod of Whitby it was resolved to follow the Roman Church practice in the calculation of Easter and in other matters of divergence between the two Churches, and although St Colman and his followers refused to bow to this decision and forsook Lindisfarne, this did not mean a total defeat and eclipse of the Celtic Church, for its spirit lived on and much was achieved through it in the ensuing years.

St Eata and St Cuthbert lived in the spirit of the Celtic Church. Then towards the end of the century the famous Lindisfarne Gospels were written down by Eadfrith, Bishop of Lindisfarne from 698 to 721.

The epoch of Theodore, Archbishop of Canterbury (669–690) saw the expansion and consolidation of the Roman Church throughout England. The Synod of Whitby was a milestone in this general movement. The influence and power of the Roman Church was inexorably flowing northward from Canterbury, all through Northumbria and westward into Galloway until it could link up with Whithorn which had remained a Christian foundation since the time of its founder St Ninian, and bringing Whithorn again within the diocese of York as it had been in Roman times. This epoch was one of building of churches, of organization of new bishoprics and parishes, of the spread of Benedictine monasteries, of the consolidation of doctrine and a codification of penances.

The flourishing of ecclesiastical activity continued after Theodore's death right up to the end of the next century, when the pagan Danes and Norsemen wreaked havoc upon the coasts of

Britain, wrecking, looting and destroying churches and monasteries.

St Bede

Ecgfrith was King of Northumbria when Bede was born in 673 or 674 and St Eata was Bishop of Lindisfarne. When Bede was seven years old, he came under Abbot St Benedict Biscop who had founded the great monasteries of Wearmouth and Jarrow. At twenty-nine Bede was ordained priest. His whole life apart from a very few journeys to collect material for his work was spent in these two monasteries. There he wrote and taught. He was the first English historian, and most of what we know of his era and of the time after the departure of the Romans is due to him. But although Bede is now famous for his *Historia Ecclesiastica Gentis Anglorum* ('Ecclesiastical History of the English People'), he wrote many other books which were copied and circulated throughout the monasteries of Europe in his own day and thereafter. He died in the summer of 735 while Ceowulf was King of Northumbria, but was declared a saint only in 1899.

Aidan and Oswald

Bede, *Ecclesiastical History,* Book III, Chapter 1

The immediate successors of King Edwin abandon the faith of their people, and Oswald, a most Christian king, restores both kingdoms

After Edwin's death in battle, the throne of Deira, the kingdom to which his ancestors had belonged and where his reign had begun, passed to a son of his uncle Aelfric; his name was Osric, and he had received the mysteries of the Christian faith during the mission of Paulinus. But the kingdom of Bernicia, the other ancient division of Northumbria, passed to Eanfrith, son of Aethelfrith, who claimed descent from its royal family. Throughout Edwin's reign the sons of this Aethelfrith, his predecessor, were living in exile with a large company of young nobles among the Irish and the Picts, and while there they were instructed in the faith as taught by the Irish and regenerated by the grace of baptism. On the death of their enemy the king they were allowed to return to their own country, and the eldest of them, Eanfrith, as we have mentioned, became king of Bernicia. Both of these kings no sooner gained the crown of their earthly kingdom than they forswore and betrayed the mysteries of the Kingdom of Heaven into which they had been initiated, and surrendered themselves again to defilement and destruction in the filthy practice of idolatry.

Before long both were slain by Cadwalla, king of the Britons, and met their just retribution at the hand of a heathen. First, the following summer he killed Osric, who had rashly laid siege to him in a fortified town. Cadwalla suddenly broke out with all his men, caught Osric unprepared, and destroyed him and his entire army. He then occupied the Northumbrian kingdoms for a whole year, not like a victorious king assuming ownership but like a cruel tyrant ravaging and tearing them apart with dreadful loss of life. Finally, when Eanfrith imprudently came to sue for peace with an escort of only twelve thanes, he visited the same fate upon him. Even today that remains an ill-omened year and hateful to all good people, both because of the apostasy of the English kings who cast aside the mysteries of the faith, and because of the savage tyranny of the king of the Britons. Consequently all those who calculate the dates of the kings have agreed to expunge the memory of the apostate kings and to assign that year to the reign of their successor, Oswald, a man beloved of God. After the murder of his brother Eanfrith Oswald arrived with an army small in numbers but protected by their faith in Christ, and he slew the accursed leader of the Britons and all that vast army that he boasted none could resist, at a place called in English Denisesburn, meaning the stream of Denise.

Bede, *Ecclesiastical History,* Book III, Chapter 2

Countless miracles of healing are wrought by the wood of the cross which Oswald had set up on going into battle against the heathen

On approaching this battle Oswald set up the sign of the holy cross and on bended knees besought God to send heavenly succour to his worshippers in the hour of their need; and the place is pointed out to this day and held in great reverence. Indeed it is said that when the cross had been quickly made and a hole made ready for it to stand in, Oswald himself, fired by his faith, seized it and placed it in its hole and held it upright with both hands, until the soldiers heaped up the soil and made it fast in the ground. Thereupon he raised his voice and cried aloud to the whole army: 'Let us all kneel, and together pray the almighty, ever-living and true God to defend us by His mercy

35

from a proud and cruel enemy; for He knows that the war we have engaged in for the deliverance of our people is a just war.' They all did as he had ordered and, advancing thus against the enemy as dawn appeared, won the victory as the reward for their faith. At the place where they prayed countless miracles of healing are known to have been wrought, a sure proof and memorial of the king's faith. To this day many visitors cut off splinters of wood from the holy cross and put them in water, which they either give to drink or sprinkle upon sick people or beasts; and these are quickly restored to health.

The place is called in English Hefenfelth, meaning Heaven's Field, a name given it in ancient times in evident anticipation of what was to come; for it signified that Heaven's standard was to be set up there, Heaven's victory won, and Heaven's miracles to continue unceasing to the present time. It lies to the north near the wall with which the Romans, as we have described earlier, encompassed the whole of Britain from sea to sea to protect it against barbarian attacks. It was in this place that the brothers of the nearby church of Hagustaldesea long ago established the custom of gathering each year on the eve of the anniversary of King Oswald's death and holding a vigil for the salvation of his soul; and on the following morning they would sing many psalms of praise and offer the holy sacrifice and oblation on his behalf. As the fame of this good custom has spread, they have lately built a church on the site and made the place more sacred and esteemed than any other in the eyes of all men. This is as it should be, for as far as we know there was no symbol of the Christian faith, no church, and no altar erected anywhere in the land of Bernicia until their new leader in war, inspired by his zeal for the faith, set up this standard of the holy cross before doing battle with his monstrous enemy.

It is not out of place to describe one of the many miracles that have been performed at this cross. A few years ago, one of the brothers of the church of Hagustaldesea, named Bothelm, who is still alive, was walking at night on the ice without proper care and suddenly fell and broke his arm. The fracture caused him great distress, as the pain prevented him even from moving his arm towards his mouth. Hearing one day that one of the brothers had arranged to go up to the site of the holy cross, he asked him to bring him on his return a piece of the venerable wood, telling him that he believed this could be the means of his recovery, if the Lord granted it. The other did as he was asked and, returning in the evening when the brothers were now seated at dinner, he presented him with a piece of the ancient moss which covered the surface of the wood. Bothelm was sitting at the table and had nothing to hand in which to keep safe the proffered gift, and so he put it in his habit; and when he went to bed he forgot to take it out and allowed it to stay there. Waking up in the middle of the night he felt something cold lying by his side, and when he moved his hand to find what it was he discovered that his arm and hand were as sound as if they had never pained him.

Bede, *Ecclesiastical History,* Book III, Chapter 3

King Oswald asks the Irish for a bishop and Aidan is sent to him; he gives aidan an episcopal see on the Island of Lindisfarne

As soon as Oswald came to the throne, he was anxious that all the people under his rule should be filled with the grace of the Christian faith, whose power he had experienced to the full in his victory over the heathen. So he sent to the Irish elders, from whom he and his escort had received the sacrament of baptism when in exile, and asked them to send him a bishop, by whose teaching and ministry the English people that he ruled might learn the blessings of faith in the Lord and receive the sacraments. He obtained his request without delay, and was sent Bishop Aidan, a man of great gentleness, holiness and moderation, who had a

zeal for God, though not wholly in accordance
with knowledge. In the fashion of his people,
which we have often referred to, he used to observe Easter Sunday between the fourteenth and
the twentieth day of the moon. The northern
province of the Irish and the whole nation of the
Picts were still celebrating Easter in that style,
believing that they followed in that observance the
writings of Anatolius, a holy and respected father of
the Church. The truth of this anyone with knowledge will determine without difficulty. But the
Irish peoples who lived in the southern parts of
Ireland learned long before to observe Easter
according to canonical custom, in obedience to the
ruling of the bishop of the Apostolic See.

When the bishop arrived, the king granted him
the island of Lindisfarne, as he requested, to be his
episcopal see. With the ebb and flow of the tide,
this is a place that is twice a day encircled by the
waves of the sea, like an island, and twice rejoined
to the mainland when its shore becomes exposed
again. In all matters Oswald listened humbly and
joyfully to the bishop's advice, and showed great
concern to build up and extend the Church of
Christ within his kingdom. The bishop was not
fully conversant with the English language, and on
many occasions it was delightful to watch while he
preached the gospel, and the king himself, having
acquired a perfect knowledge of Irish during his

long exile, acted as interpreter of Heaven's word for his aldermen and thanes.

From that time many missionaries from Irish territory began to arrive in Britain as the days went by, who preached the word of the faith with great zeal to the English kingdoms ruled over by Oswald; and to those who believed, such of them as held the rank of priest administered the grace of baptism. Churches were built in various places, and the people gladly flocked together to hear the Word. By the gift of the king, estates and lands were granted for the establishment of monasteries, and English boys together with their elders were given systematic instruction by Irish teachers and taught to observe the discipline of a Rule.

For those who came to preach were mostly monks. Bishop Aidan himself was a monk; he was sent from the island of Hii, whose monastery was for a long time chief among most of the northern Irish and all the Picts, exercising control over their peoples. This island belongs to Britain, being separated from it by a narrow strait, but was long ago given to Irish monks by the Picts who inhabit that part of Britain, because it was through the monks' preaching that they adopted the Christian faith.

Bede, *Ecclesiastical History,* Book III, Chapter 4

The Picts receive the Christian faith

In the year of our Lord 565, when Justin the Younger succeeded Justinianus as ruler of the Roman Empire, there came to Britain from Ireland a priest and abbot named Columba, a true monk in his life as in his habit, to preach the word of God to the kingdoms of the northern Picts; these people are separated from the southern territories of the Picts by a range of steep and rugged mountains. The southern Picts themselves, whose homes are on this side of these mountains, are said to have given up the errors of idolatry long before this and received the true faith through the preaching of the word by Bishop Ninian, a most reverend and holy man of British race, who had received orthodox instruction at Rome in the mysteries of the true faith. His episcopal see, distinguished by its church dedicated to St Martin, where his body rests together with many other saints, is now under the rule of the English. The place is part of the kingdom of Bernicia and popularly known as the White House, because Ninian built a church of stone there, a style of building unfamiliar to the Britons.

Now Columba came to Britain in the ninth year of the reign of Bruide, son of Maelchon, a Pictish king of great power, and converted the people to the Christian faith by his word and his example; and because of this they gave him possession of the island mentioned above to build a monastery. It is a small island, about five hides in area according to English reckoning, and his successors live there to this day. Columba himself was buried there, having died at the age of seventy-seven about thirty-two years after coming to preach in Britain. Before coming to Britain he had built a noble monastery in Ireland, called Dearmach in the Irish language, meaning the field of the oaks, after the many oak trees that stand there. His disciples from both of these monasteries went on to found many more monasteries in Britain and in Ireland, over all of which the island monastery, where his body lies at rest, held pre-eminence.

The island itself always has as its ruler an abbot in priest's orders, to whose jurisdiction the whole province, including even the bishops, is subject. This unusual arrangement follows the precedent of their first teacher, who was not a bishop but a priest and a monk. It is said that his disciples possess some written records of his life and teaching, but whatever type of man he may have been, we know for certain that he left to succeed him men distinguished by great abstinence, a love of God, and observance of the Rule. It is true that they followed unreliable calculations of the date of the greatest Christian festival, as they lived at the far ends of the earth and no one had acquainted them with the synodal decrees about the observance of Easter; but they diligently practised those works of devotion and purity which they could learn from the writings of the prophets, evangelists and apostles. They persisted in this reckoning of the date of Easter for a considerable time, a hundred and fifty years in fact, until the year of our Lord 715.

In that year, however, they were visited by Egbert, of English race, a most reverend and holy father and bishop, who had for long been an exile in Ireland for the sake of Christ, and was most learned in the scriptures and famed for his long and saintly life; and they were set right by him and converted to the true and canonical date of Easter. Previously, they did not always follow the Jewish practice, as some supposed, and observe it on the fourteenth day of the moon; they always observed Easter on a Sunday, but in the wrong week. As Christians they knew that the resurrection of the Lord, which occurred on the day after the Sabbath, must always be celebrated on the day after the Sabbath; but being an uncivilized and ignorant people they had never learned when that first day after the Sabbath, now called the Lord's Day, should occur. Even so, because the grace of Christian love never failed to inspire them, they were accounted worthy of full knowledge of this matter also, in accordance with the promise of the apostle when he says: 'And if in anything ye be otherwise minded, God shall reveal even this unto you.' We shall have more to say on this subject in its proper place in the pages that follow.

Bede, *Ecclesiastical History*, Book III, Chapter 5

The life of Bishop Aidan

It was from this island, then, and this community of monks that Aidan was sent after his consecration as bishop to instruct the English kingdom in the faith of Christ, at the time when Seghine, abbot and priest, was in charge of the monastery. Among the lessons that Aidan had given the clergy about the conduct of their lives there was none more salutary than his own example of abstinence and self-discipline; and his teaching commended itself to everyone above all because he taught the way of life that he and his followers practised. He neither sought nor cared for the possessions of this world, and he took delight in giving away to poor people whom he met all the gifts he received from kings and rich men of the world. He used to travel everywhere, whether in town or in the country, not on horseback but on foot, unless forced to do otherwise by some urgent necessity, so that wherever as he walked he caught sight of people, rich or poor, he could at once turn and speak to them. If they were unbelievers he would invite them to accept the mystery of the faith; while those who already believed he would strengthen in the faith and encourage by his words and actions in the practice of almsgiving and works of mercy.

His way of life was in great contrast to the slothfulness of our own times, so much so that all who travelled with him, whether tonsured or laymen, were required to study, that is to occupy themselves in reading the scriptures or learning the psalms. This was the daily task of Aidan and all his company wherever they went. If it chanced, as it seldom did, that he was summoned to feast with the king, he attended with one or two of his clergy, and after a little refreshment made haste to leave to continue reading with his followers, or else to pray. Inspired by his example many devout men and women at that time formed the habit of prolonging their fast on Wednesday and Friday until the ninth hour, except for the period between Easter and Pentecost. If wealthy people did wrong he never kept silent out of deference or fear, but would correct them with a stern rebuke. He never gave money to powerful men of the world, but only food to such as he entertained; and those gifts of money that he received from the rich he preferred to distribute for the use of the poor, as we have said, or spend in ransoming people unjustly sold into slavery. In fact many of those he had ransomed later became his disciples, and after training and instructing them he ordained them to the priesthood.

It is said that when King Oswald asked the Irish for a bishop to teach the faith to him and his people, another man of sterner temperament was sent at first; but although he preached among the English for some time he met with no success, and the people were unwilling to listen to him. He therefore returned home and announced at a meeting of the elders that he had been able to make no headway in teaching the nation to which he had been sent, for they were an intractable people of stubborn and uncivilized character. They are said to have held a long discussion at their conference on what should be done, as they wished to bring to that people the salvation they sought, while regretting that the preacher they had sent had not been welcomed. Then Aidan, who was at the meeting himself, said to the priest in question: 'It seems to me, brother, that you have been unduly severe with your ignorant hearers. You should have followed the guidance of the apostle and offered them at first the milk of simpler teaching, until gradually, growing strong on the food of God's word, they could take in a fuller statement of the faith and carry out God's more exalted commands.'

When they heard this, everyone present turned to look at Aidan, and after careful consideration of the meaning of his words, they resolved that it was he who should be made bishop and sent to instruct an unbelieving and ignorant people, because he had proved himself to be endowed above all with the grace of discretion, which is the mother of all the virtues; and so they consecrated him and sent him to preach. As time went on he showed himself to be blessed not only with that discretion and good sense but with the other virtues also.

Bede, *Ecclesiastical History,* Book III, Chapter 6

The wonderful devotion and piety of King Oswald

Such then was the bishop who gave instruction in the faith to King Oswald and the English nation that he ruled; and Oswald not only learned to hope for a kingdom in Heaven unknown to his ancestors, but also gained a greater earthly kingdom than any of his predecessors, from the same one God who made Heaven and earth. In fact he brought under his control all the peoples and kingdoms of Britain, speaking between them four different languages, British, Pictish, Irish and English.

Yet it is wonderful to relate of one elevated to such a height of kingly power, that he was always humble, kind and generous towards the poor and towards strangers. For example, it is said that once on Easter Day when he was sitting at dinner with the bishop, and a silver dish was placed before him on the table full of royal fare, they were about to raise their hands to ask a blessing on the bread when one of his officers, whose duty it was to bring relief to the needy, suddenly came in and told the king that a large crowd of poor people from every district was sitting in the precincts, asking for alms from the king. He at once ordered the meal that had been served to him to be taken out to the poor, and the dish to be broken in pieces and divided among them. When he saw it, the bishop who sat with him was delighted by the act of mercy, and took his right hand and said: 'May this hand never wither with age.' And his prayer and blessing were fulfilled, for when Oswald was killed in battle his hand and arm were severed from his body, and they remain undecayed to this day. They are preserved in the royal town named after Bebba a former queen, stored in a silver casket in the church of St Peter, and are venerated with due honour by everyone.

Through the efforts of this king the kingdoms of Deira and Bernicia, which were previously at enmity with each other, were peacefully united and became one people. Oswald was the nephew of King Edwin through his sister Acha, and it was fitting that so great a predecessor should have such a kinsman to inherit both his religion and his throne.

Bede, *Ecclesiastical History,* Book III, Chapter 9

At the place where Oswald was killed many miracles of healing occur

Oswald, that most Christian king of Northumbria, reigned for nine years, including that year which had been made an object of loathing by the unholy savagery of the king of the Britons and the insane apostasy of the English kings. For, as we have explained above, it was decided by general agreement that the name and memory of the apostates should be wholly expunged from the list of Christian kings, and no year assigned to their reign. At the end of this period Oswald was killed in a great battle against the same heathen people, the Mercians, and their heathen king, as had slain his predecessor Edwin. The date was the fifth of August, and he was thirty-eight years old. The place where he died is called in English Maserfelth. ...

King Oswin was tall and handsome, a man of pleasant conversation and courteous manners, and open-handed to people of high and low birth alike;

as a result he was loved by everyone for the royal dignity which showed itself in his character, his bearing and his actions, and noblemen from almost every kingdom came together to serve in his retinue. He was graced and, one might say, especially blessed with the virtues that spring from self-denial and with none, it is said, more than humility, as a single example will show.

He had given an excellent horse to Bishop Aidan so that, although it was his custom to walk, he could ride it when he had to cross rivers or some other urgent necessity arose. Not long afterwards Aidan was met by a poor man begging for alms, and dismounted and ordered the horse, complete with its royal trappings, to be given to the beggar; for he was a man of great compassion and a friend of the poor, and like a father to those in need. When the king was told of this, he said to the bishop as they were going in to dinner: 'My Lord Bishop, why did you want to give the royal horse to a beggar? It would have been better for you to keep it as your own. Did we not have many less valuable horses, and other things which would have been good enough to give to the poor, without giving away the horse that I chose especially for your own use?' The bishop replied at once: 'What are you saying, Your Majesty? Surely that son of a mare is not more dear to you than that son of God?' With this, they went in to dinner. The bishop sat in his place, but the king, who had been hunting, stood by the fire with his thanes to get warm. As he warmed himself he remembered what the bishop had said to him, and suddenly unbuckled his sword and gave it to a thane, and then made haste to fall at the bishop's feet to ask his pardon. 'Never again,' he said, 'will I speak of this or pass judgement on what wealth of mine you should give to God's sons.' When the bishop saw this he was greatly alarmed, and stood up and lifted the king to his feet, assuring him that all was forgiven if only he would take his seat at dinner and banish his sorrow. The king, at the bishop's urgent bidding, recovered his good spirits, but the bishop for his part grew so sad that he burst into tears. He was asked by a priest in his native language, which the king and his retainers did not understand, why he wept, and said: 'I know that the king has not long to live. I have never before seen a humble king, and I therefore expect that he will soon be taken from this life; for this nation does not deserve to have such a ruler.' Not long after, the bishop's grim prophecy was fulfilled, as we have described, by the sad death of the king.

Bishop Aidan himself was taken from this world only eleven days after the murder of the king he loved, on the thirty-first of August, and received from the Lord the everlasting reward of his labours.

Bede, *Ecclesiastical History,* Book III, Chapter 15

*Bishop Aidan foretells a storm to some sailors, and
gives them holy oil with which to calm it*

The God who judges our hearts revealed by miraculous signs how great was Aidan's worth, and it
will be sufficient to put on record three of them. A
priest named Utta, a most sincere and honest man
and for that reason honoured by all, including the
rulers of this world, was once sent to Kent to bring
Eanfled, daughter of King Edwin, to marry King
Oswy; she had been taken to Kent after her father's
death. The priest intended to travel there by land
but to return with the maiden by sea, and went to
Bishop Aidan to beg him to pray to the Lord for
his companions and himself at the start of their
long journey. Aidan blessed them and commended
them to the Lord, and also gave them some holy
oil. 'I know,' he said, 'that when you have em-
barked on your ship a storm and adverse wind will
rise up against you. But you, father, remember to
pour this oil that I give you on to the sea, and then
the winds will at once be stilled and you will enjoy
a calm sea to return home by the way you wish.'
All this happened just as the bishop had foretold.
At first the waves of the sea were wild and the
sailors tried to secure the ship by casting anchor,
but all to no purpose. The waves swept over the

ship from all sides and began to fill it, and everyone saw that death was at hand and expected to perish at any moment. Just then the priest, remembering the bishop's words, took the flask and poured the oil into the sea, and at once, as he foretold, its fury was stilled. So it came to pass that the man of God foretold the storm by the spirit of prophecy, and by the power of the same spirit made it calm again, though absent in body. I received the account of this miracle not from any unreliable source but from a most trustworthy priest of our church named Cynemund, who said that he had heard it from the priest Utta himself, on whom and through whom it was accomplished.

Bede, *Ecclesiastical History,* Book III, Chapter 16

The enemy attack the royal town with fire, but Aidan saves it by prayer

Many people who were in a position to know tell of another miracle concerning St Aidan. During the time of his episcopate an enemy army of Mercians led by Penda laid waste the land of Northumbria far and wide with godless destruction, until they reached the royal town named after the former queen Bebba. They could not capture the town either by assault or by siege, and so attempted to destroy it by fire. They tore apart the small hamlets that they found in the neighbourhood and carried to the town a great mass of beams, rafters, partition walls, wattle and thatch, which they piled high round the wall on its landward side. When they saw the wind to be favourable, they started a fire in an attempt to burn down the town. At that time the most reverend Bishop Aidan was staying on Farne Island, about two miles from the town. He often used to go into retreat there to spend time in silent prayer, and in fact the site of his solitary dwelling is pointed out to this day. When he saw the tongues of fire and the smoke being carried by the wind over the town walls, he is said to have looked up to Heaven in tears and raised his hands, saying: 'See, Lord, the great evil that Penda does.' At these words the wind at once changed direction away from the town and hurled back the flames upon those who had kindled them. Some were injured and all were terrified, and they abandoned further assault on the town, realizing that it was under divine protection.

Bede, *Ecclesiastical History,* Book III, Chapter 17

*The buttress of the church on which he was leaning
when he died cannot be destroyed by the flames when
the rest of the building is on fire; his spiritual life*

When the day arrived for him to depart this life
after seventeen years as bishop, Aidan was on a
royal estate not far from the town of which we
have been speaking. He had a church and a cell
there where he often used to stay, going out to
preach in the surrounding countryside. This was his
custom on other royal estates, where he had no
property of his own except his church with its
small plot of land. When he fell ill, therefore, they
erected a tent for him at the west end of the
church so that it was actually attached to the
church wall; and so it came about that he breathed
his last leaning on a buttress which supported the
church on the outside. He died in the seventeenth
year of his episcopate, on the thirty-first of August.
His body was taken across shortly afterwards to the
island of Lindisfarne and buried in the brothers'
cemetery; but some time later, when a larger
church had been built there, consecrated in honour
of the most blessed chief of the apostles, his bones
were transferred to it and buried on the right of
the altar with the respect due to so great a bishop.

He was succeeded as bishop by Finan, who was

also sent from the Irish island monastery of Hii, and who held office for a considerable time. A few years later Penda, king of the Mercians, invaded the region, destroying everything he could by fire and sword, and the village in which Aidan died, including the church, was burnt down. But, miraculously, only the buttress on which he was leaning when he died could not be destroyed by the flames, though they devoured everything around it. When the miracle became known, the church was quickly rebuilt on the same spot and the same buttress used to support the wall on the outside as before. Some time afterwards it again happened that the village together with the church was destroyed by fire, this time through carelessness. But on that occasion also the flames were powerless to touch the buttress, and it was a great miracle indeed that, while they licked through the very nail-holes by which it was attached to the building, they were not permitted to damage it in any way. Consequently, when a third church was built there they set up that buttress not, as before, outside as a support for the building, but inside the church itself in memory of the miracle, so that those who came in might kneel and pray for Heaven's mercy. It is well known that from that time many people have obtained the grace of healing at that place; and many also by cutting off splinters from the buttress and putting them in water, have found it a means of curing the ailments of themselves and their families.

I have written this account of Aidan's character and life without in any way commending or approving his inaccurate knowledge of the observance of Easter. On the contrary, this is something that I abhor, as I have shown very clearly in my book on chronology; but as a truthful historian I have given a straightforward account of his deeds and of events associated with him, giving praise where due to his way of life and setting it on record for the benefit of my readers. He cultivated peace and love, self-discipline and humility. His heart had the mastery over anger and avarice, and was contemptuous of pride and vainglory. He spared no effort in carrying out and teaching the commands of Heaven, and was diligent in his reading and keeping of vigils. He showed the authority befitting a bishop in rebuking the proud and mighty, and was merciful in bringing comfort to the weak and relief and protection to the poor. In brief, as far as we have discovered from those who knew him, he neglected none of the duties that he learned from the writings of the evangelists, apostles and prophets, but strove with all his strength to fulfil them in his life. For these qualities the bishop wins my heartfelt admiration, since I know them to have been pleasing to God. However, as to his habit of observing Easter at the wrong time, whether in ignorance of the canonical time or because, though aware of it, he disregarded it out of deference to his race, this I neither approve nor commend. This much, even so, I can approve; that in the celebration of his own Easter he had at heart the same faith, and worshipped and preached the same mystery as we, namely the redemption of the human race through the passion, resurrection and ascension into Heaven of the one mediator between God and men, even the man Christ Jesus. This is why he did not, as some wrongly suppose, follow the Jews in keeping Easter on the fourteenth day of the moon whatever the day, but always kept it on the Lord's Day between the fourteenth and the twentieth day of the moon: he had faith in the Lord's resurrection, which he believed to have occurred on the day after the Sabbath, and hope of our resurrection, which he was convinced would also occur on the day after the Sabbath, now known as the Lord's Day. In these beliefs he was at one with holy Church.

The Life of St Cuthbert by an Anonymous Author

– Book I –

A prologue concerning obedience

I would that the result of my obedience to your commands, O holy bishop Eadfrith, and to the commands of the whole community might be as good as my intentions. For this is a great task for me and my powers of understanding are small. But, so far as I am concerned, even if I am over-whelmed by the amount of sacred material at my disposal, yet I am satisfied that I have not failed in obedience to the commands you laid upon my powers ... And I beg you, if anything has turned out otherwise than you wished, that balancing fairly my weakness against the task imposed, you will judge the labour of my imperfect enterprise in terms of duty rather than of merit. But, if I produce anything worthy of your reading, it will assuredly be by the help of divine grace. Who will fail to understand that the task undertaken was one which you believe even me capable of carrying through with the help of your prayers? So with great joy I undertook your loving command. For this record of St Cuthbert is of great gain and value to myself. Indeed it is in itself a ready path to virtue to know what he was. ...

Preface to the writing

I will therefore undertake to write the life of St Cuthbert and how he lived both before and after he became bishop; yet I have not been able to find out all his miracles by any means; for those which he alone was aware of are unknown, because, as he did not seek the praise of men, he desired that all his miracles should be hidden so far as this was in his power. Yet we have omitted many, even, of those which were known to us, because we believed that it would be sufficient if only the more outstanding ones were noted, and at the same time, we had to consider our readers, lest too plentiful an abundance might produce in them a feeling of distaste. So I beseech my readers to believe my report and not to think that I have written anything except what has been received on good authority and tested. Nay, I would rather hold my peace than state what is false. But since, assuredly, neither the written nor the spoken word can do justice to all his numerous works, let us start upon an account of his deeds.

How a child prophesied concerning him

First we record an incident of his early youth, known to us through the reports of many, among whom are Bishop Tumma of holy memory, who learnt from St Cuthbert's own lips that God's choice of him to a spiritual office had been pre-determined, and Elias also, a priest of our church. These tell the story thus. When he was a boy of eight years, he surpassed all of his age in agility and high spirits, so that often, after the others had gone to rest their weary limbs, he, standing triumphantly in the playground as though he were in the arena, would still wait for someone to play with him. At that time many youths were gathered together one day on a piece of level ground and he too was found among them. They began thereupon to indulge in a variety of games and tricks; some of them stood naked, with their heads turned down unnaturally towards the ground, their legs stretched out and their feet lifted up and pointing skywards; and some did one thing and some another.

Now among them there was a certain child scarcely three years old who began to call out to him repeatedly: 'Be steadfast and leave this foolish play.' Seeing his commands disregarded, he thereupon wailed and wept and became almost inconsolable. At last being asked what was the matter with him, he began to cry out: 'O holy Bishop and priest Cuthbert, these unnatural tricks done to show off your agility are not befitting to you or your high office.'

Cuthbert did not clearly understand, but he nevertheless gave up his vain games and began to console the child; and returning home, he kept in mind the prophetic words, just as St Mary kept in her memory all the words which were prophesied about Jesus. Behold, brethren, how even before he is recognized by the performance of his works, he is shown by the providence of God to be elect; even as it is said concerning the patriarch by the prophet: 'Jacob have I loved but Esau have I hated.' Samuel and David also are both found to have been chosen in their infancy. The prophet Jeremiah too and John the Baptist are said to have been sanctified for the work of the Lord from their mother's womb. So the teacher of the Gentiles affirmed, saying: 'Whom he did predestinate, them he also called' and so forth.

How he was healed by an angel

While he was still the same age, the Lord by another miracle honoured him as one who had been predestined by the election of God. For when he was a boy, as I have said, and still of the laity, he was laid up with an infirmity which pressed cruelly upon him. His knee swelled, his sinews contracted, and he became so lame that one foot was unable to touch the ground.

Once, when he had been carried outside and was lying near the wall in the warmth of the sun, he saw a man of noble appearance and of wondrous beauty, clad in white robes, come riding up to him from afar, upon a magnificently caparisoned horse. When he drew near, he saluted the boy with words of peace and asked him if he was willing to minister to him as a guest.

Cuthbert, showing him his bodily infirmity, answered fearlessly, 'If it had been God's will and if He had not bound me with the bonds of infirmity on account of my sins, I would not be slow to minister to guests in his honour.' The man thereupon descended from his horse and examining his knee which, as Cuthbert had already explained, no doctor had tended, gave him these instructions: 'You must cook wheat flour with milk, and anoint your knee with it, while it is hot.'

After the man had gone, the boy obeyed his command, perceiving that he was an angel of God. After a few days he was healed according to his faith, and gave thanks to God who had shown him pity and had completely cured him through the ministration of his angel, even as He had healed

Tobias when he was blind. And from that time, as he revealed to men who can be fully trusted, whenever he prayed to the Lord in the times of his greatest distress, he was never denied the help of angels.

– Book II –

Of the beginning of his life in the service of God

So having arranged to bind himself by the more rigid rule of life in a monastery, leaving his secular life, pious and undefiled though it was, he advanced to better things and patiently bore the holy labour for, by long-standing zeal for voluntary bond service in the work of God and by custom, it had become part of his nature. He was able to endure such fastings and such watchings that his strength silenced unbelief. He very often spent the whole night in prayer, sometimes even enduring a second and a third night, and refreshed himself only on the fourth day, remembering the words of the Apostle Paul, 'Now no chastening for the present seemeth to be joyous but grievous; nevertheless afterwards it yieldeth the peaceable fruit of righteousness to them that are exercised thereby.'

O brethren, I do not assume that I am worthy to tell his life, nay rather, no man's words can describe it. For he was angelic in appearance, refined in conversation, holy in works, unblemished in body, noble in nature, mighty in counsel, orthodox in faith, patient in hope, wide in charity. Let me, nevertheless, make clear the course of his miracles.

How he ministered to an angel and was given three loaves by God

Now this was another miracle in which Cuthbert the holy man of God was first glorified by the Lord, after he had by the Lord's help taken upon him the yoke of bondservice to Christ and the Petrine tonsure after the shape of the crown of thorns that bound the head of Christ, in the monastery which is called Ripon.

This miracle our most trustworthy witnesses who are still alive have testified to. For while a neophyte, he was at once elected by the community to minister to guests on their arrival. Among these, on the morning of a certain day when the weather was wintry and snowy, an angel of the Lord appeared to him in the form of a well-built man in the flower of his age, just as angels appeared to the patriarch Abraham in the valley of Mamre in the form of men. Then having received him kindly in accordance with his wont, still thinking him to be a man and not an angel, he washed his hands and feet and wiped them with towels, and, having in his humility rubbed his guest's feet with his own hands to warm them on account of the cold, he invited him most urgently to wait until the third hour of the day to take food; but he was unwilling and refused on account of his journey. Finally Cuthbert adjured him in the name of our Lord Jesus Christ and so won his consent.

When the signal was given at the third hour of the day and prayer was over, he at once set out a table and spread thereon such food as he had. Now by some chance there was no bread in the guest-house, save that he had placed some crumbs on the table as a blessed gift of bread. Thereupon the man of God went back to the monastery to seek a loaf; but failing to get any (for they were still baking in the oven) he returned to the guest whom he had left eating alone; but he did not find him nor even his footprints although there was snow over the surface of the ground. He was amazed and re-moved the table to the store house, realizing that it was an angel of God. And immediately at the entrance, his nostrils were filled with the odour of the choicest bread and, finding three warm loaves, he gave thanks to God, because in him was fulfilled the saying of the Lord: 'He that receiveth you receiveth me, and he that receiveth me receiveth him that sent me,' and again: 'He that receiveth a prophet in the name of a prophet shall receive a prophet's reward, and he that receiveth a righteous man in the name of a righteous man shall receive a righteous man's reward.' And frequently from that day, when he was hungry, the Lord fed him, as he used to declare to faithful brethren, not boastfully, but for the edification of many, just as Paul told many things about himself.

How the sea animals ministered to him and how a brother who tested him was healed

And this incident I think should also be related, which I learned from the account of many good men, among whom is Plecgils a priest, at the time when he was in the monastery which we call Melrose; Cuthbert was sent for by the nun Aebbe, a widow, and the mother of them all in Christ. He came to the monastery which is called Coldingham, in response to the invitation, and remaining there some days, did not relax his habitual way of life but began to walk about by night on the seashore, keeping up his custom of singing as he kept vigil.

When a certain cleric of the community found this out, he began to follow him from a distance to test him, wishing to know what he did with himself at night. But that man of God, approaching the sea with mind made resolute, went into the waves up to his loin-cloth; and once he was soaked as far as his armpits by the tumultuous and stormy sea. Then coming up out of the sea, he prayed, bending his knees on the sandy part of the shore, and immediately there followed in his footsteps two little sea animals, humbly prostrating themselves on the earth; and, licking his feet, they rolled upon them, wiping them with their skins and warming them with their breath. After this service and ministry had been fulfilled and his blessing had been received, they departed to their haunts in the waves of the sea.

But the man of God, returning home at cock-crow, came to the church of God to join in public prayer with the brethren. The above-mentioned cleric of the community lay hidden amid the rocks, frightened and trembling at the sight and, being in anguish all night long, he came nigh to death. The next day he prostrated himself before the feet of the man of God and, in a tearful voice, prayed for his pardon and indulgence. The man of God answered him with prophetic words: 'My brother, what is the matter with you? Have you approached nearer me, to test me, than you should have done? Nevertheless, since you admit it, you shall receive pardon on one condition; that you vow never to tell the story so long as I am alive.'

The brother made the vow and kept it after-wards and departed with his blessing, healed. But after Cuthbert's death he told many brethren how

the animals ministered to the saint, just as we read
in the Old Testament that the lions ministered to
Daniel, and related how Cuthbert, to his amaze-
ment, had seen him with his spiritual eyes, when
he was lying hid and testing him, just as Peter
detected Ananias and Sapphira when they were
tempting the Holy Spirit.

*Concerning the dolphin flesh which the lord provided
for him and concerning his prophecy*

At another time also, he went from the same
monastery which is called Melrose with two
brothers, and, setting sail for the land of the Picts,
they reached the land called the region of the
Niduari in safety. They remained there some days
in great want, for hunger afflicted them and the
tempestuous sea prevented them from continuing
their voyage. But the man of God, after spending
the night near the shore in prayer, came to them in
the morning of the day of the Epiphany of the
Lord, for they had started out after Christmas.

Thereupon he urged them saying: 'Let us go and
seek, asking God to fulfil his promise when he said:
"Ask and it shall be given to you, seek and ye shall
find, knock and it shall be opened unto you." For
I think that the Lord will give us something to
celebrate the day on which the Magi worshipped
him with gifts and on which the Holy Ghost in the

form of a dove descended upon him at his baptism in Jordan, and on which he turned water into wine in Cana of Galilee to confirm the faith of his disciples.'

They then arose and went out. He went in front of them as though he were the forerunner, until they came to the sea. And immediately they looked and found three portions of dolphin's flesh as though they had been cut by a human hand with a knife and washed with water. So the man of God, kneeling down, gave thanks to the Lord and said to his companions: 'Take them and carry them away and bless the Lord. For behold three portions are sufficient for three men for three days and three nights; but on the fourth day, the sea will be calm for sailing.'

So they took them away and cooked them and enjoyed the wonderful sweetness of the flesh. They remained three days amid a fierce tempest and on the fourth day, according to his word, they prosperously reached a port of safety after a calm voyage. So one of the two brethren mentioned above named Tydi, who is a priest and still alive, declared to us before many witnesses; and he glorified God because He then bestowed flesh upon the man of God with the same mercy as He had once bestowed it in the desert upon Elijah, and because, inspired by the same Spirit, Cuthbert foresaw the tempest and the calm, just as the Apostle Paul did in the Acts of the Apostles when he prophesied to the voyagers.

How an eagle caught a fish in accordance with the prophecy of the servant of God

Now the above-mentioned priest Tydi spoke of another miracle which is known to many. On a certain day, he was going along the river Teviot and making his way southward, teaching the country people among the mountains and baptizing them. Having a boy walking with him in his company he said to him: 'Do you think that someone has prepared you your midday meal today?' He answered that he knew of none of their kindred along that way and he did not hope for any sort of kindness from unknown strangers.

The servant of God said again to him: 'My son, be of good cheer; the Lord will provide food for those who hope in him, for he said, "seek ye first the Kingdom of God and his righteousness and all these things shall be added unto you;" in order that the saying of the prophet may be fulfilled: "I have been young and now am old, yet have I not seen the righteous forsaken," and so forth. "For the labourer is worthy of his hire." '

After some such words he looked up to heaven and saw an eagle flying in the sky and said to his boy: 'This is the eagle which the Lord has instructed to provide us with food today.' After a short time, as they went on their way, they saw the eagle settling on the bank of the river. The boy ran towards the eagle in accordance with the command of the servant of God, and stopping, he found a large fish. The boy brought the whole of it to him, whereupon Cuthbert said: 'Why did you not give our fisherman a part of it to eat since he was fasting?' Then the boy, in accordance with the commands of the man of God, gave half of the fish to the eagle while they took the other half with them, and broiling it in the company of some men, they ate it, and gave some to the others and were satisfied, worshipping the Lord and giving thanks. Then they set out according to God's will to the mountains, as we have said above, teaching and baptizing the people in the name of the Father and of the Son and of the Holy Ghost.

– Book III –

How, living according to the scriptures, he finally took to a solitary life on an island and there cut himself a place out of the rock

So St Cuthbert as prior served the Lord well in the aforesaid monastery which is called Melrose, and the Lord did more marvellous works by him than I have attempted to write down, because those that are weak in faith would hardly believe them; but finally he fled from worldly glory and sailed away privately and secretly. Then he was invited and constrained by the venerable and holy Bishop Eata and came, by God's help to this island of ours which is called Lindisfarne, where, both present and absent, he healed those possessed of devils and cured various other infirmities. He dwelt there also according to Holy Scripture, following the contemplative amid the active life, and he arranged our rule of life which we composed then for the first time and which we observe even to this day along with the rule of St Benedict.

And so, after some years, desiring a solitary life he went to the island called Farne, which is in the midst of the sea and surrounded on every side by water, a place where, before this, almost no one could remain alone for any length of time on account of the various illusions caused by devils. But he fearlessly put them to flight and, digging down almost a cubit of a man into the earth, through very hard and stony rock, he made a space to dwell in. He also built a marvellous wall another cubit above it by placing together and compacting with earth, stones of such great size as none would believe except those who knew that so much of the power of God was in him; therein he made some little dwelling-places from which he could see nothing except the heavens above.

How he prophesied the end of King Ecgfrith's life and about his heir and about his own bishopric

Furthermore there was a certain nun, a virgin and royal abbess called Aelflaed who humbly asked the hermit of God in the name of the Lord to cross the sea and meet her at Coquet Island. The hand-maiden of God on bended knees began to ask him many things and finally she adjured him boldly by the name of our Lord Jesus Christ and by the nine orders of angels and the persons of all the saints, and asked him concerning the length of life of her brother King Ecgfrith.

Now the man of God, being so solemnly adjured and fearing the Lord, began to speak in an indirect way about the brevity of man's life and added these words: 'O handmaiden of the Lord, is it not but a short time though a man were to live twelve months?' She immediately realized that he spoke of the king, and wept bitter tears; and the fall of the members of the royal house by a cruel hand and a hostile sword a year afterwards renewed all the bitterness for her and for many others.

She then added: 'By this same Unity and Trinity, I adjure you to tell me whom he will have as his heir.' He was silent for a short time and then said: 'You will find him to be a brother no less than the other one.' This indeed seemed incredible; but she asked him more carefully in what place he was. He bore with her patiently, saying: 'O hand-maiden of God, why should you wonder though he be on some island beyond this sea?' She quickly realized that he had spoken of Aldfrith who now reigns peacefully and who was then on the island which is called Iona.

She added also a question about himself, and knowing that the king had wished to offer him a bishopric, she asked if the matter would be settled thus, and how long he would be in the bishopric. He, pleading that he was not worthy and yet that neither on sea or land could he hide himself from so honourable a rank, said: 'And after the brief space of two years, I shall find a rest from my labours. And you too hearken! I bid you, in the name of our Lord Jesus Christ, tell this to no one while I live.' And after many prophetic words, all of which came to pass without fail, he sailed to his own place.

Concerning his manner of life in solitude

And so for several years he continued to live a solitary life cut off from the sight of men; and also in all conditions he bore himself with un-shaken balance, for he kept throughout the same countenance, the same spirit. At all hours he was happy and joyful, neither wearing a sad expression at the remembrance of a sin nor being elated by the loud praises of those who marvelled at his manner of life. His conversation, seasoned with salt, consoled the sad, instructed the ignorant, appeased the angry, for he persuaded them all to put nothing before the love of Christ. And he placed before the eyes of all the greatness of future benefits and the mercy of God, and revealed the favours already bestowed; namely that God spared not His own Son but delivered him up for the salvation of us all.

– Book IV –

How he was compelled by the Council to accept the bishopric

So afterwards he was elected to the bishopric of our church at Lindisfarne at the request of King Ecgfrith and the bishops of the Saxons and all the council; for at that time the above mentioned king and Bishop Tumma of holy memory and chosen men of our community came to him while he was within his cell, bearing the decision of the council, and on bended knees adjured him by our Lord Jesus Christ. So he was led away unwillingly and under compulsion, weeping and wailing, while the council together with Archbishop Theodore still awaited him.

However after a time he accepted the bishopric, and though it is not in our power to narrate how he distinguished himself, yet it is nevertheless better to describe some part than to omit the whole. For he continued with the utmost constancy to be what he had been before; he showed the same humility of heart, the same poverty of dress, and, being full of authority and grace, he maintained the dignity of a bishop without abandoning the ideal of the monk or the virtue of the hermit. In all these things he observed the teaching of the apostle Paul to Titus, remembering that he said: 'A bishop must be blameless as the steward of God, not self-willed, not soon angry, not given to wine, no striker, not quarrelsome, not given to filthy lucre, but a lover of hospitality, a lover of good, sober, just, holy, temperate; holding fast the faithful word as he hath been taught, that he may be able by sound doctrine both to exhort and to convince the gainsayers.' For his discourse was pure and frank, full of gravity and probity, full of sweetness and grace, dealing with the ministry of the law, the teaching of the faith, the virtue of temperance, and the practice of righteousness. To each one he gave varied advice with exhortation suitable to his character; that is to say he always knew beforehand what advice to give to any man and when and how it should be given.

Before everything it was his special care to take part in fastings, prayers, vigils and reading of the Scriptures. His memory served him instead of books when he rehearsed the Old and New Testaments; he followed the example of the saints, fulfilling the duty of peace among his brethren; he held fast humility also and that most excellent gift of charity without which every other virtue is nothing worth. He cared for the poor, fed the hungry, clothed the naked, took in strangers, redeemed captives, and protected widows and orphans, that he might merit the reward of eternal life amid the choirs of angels in the presence of our Lord Jesus Christ.

How he conducted himself in the bishopric

Therefore as St Cuthbert excelled in virtues in his bishopric, the Lord completely and fully increased the dignity and authority of that office through him by signs and wonders; for what we read concerning the Apostles, 'Whatsoever ye shall loose on earth,' etc. and 'Whatsoever ye shall bind on earth,' etc. was fulfilled in him with respect to men's souls and bodies; as his priests and deacons who were with him have told us. For 'many signs and wonders,' as it says in the Acts of the Apostles, 'were wrought among the people.'

Concerning the day and the hour of the slaying of King Ecgfrith

At the time when King Ecgfrith was ravaging and laying waste the kingdom of the Picts, though finally in accordance with the predestined judgment of God he was to be overcome and slain, our holy bishop went to the city of Carlisle to visit the queen who was awaiting there the issue of events.

On the Saturday, as the priests and deacons declare of whom many still survive, at the ninth hour they were looking at the city wall and the well formerly built in a wonderful manner by the Romans, as Waga the reeve of the city, who was conducting them, explained. The bishop meanwhile stood leaning on his supporting staff, with his head inclined towards the ground and then he lifted up his eyes heavenwards again with a sigh and said: 'Oh! oh! oh! I think that the war is over and that judgment has been given against our people in the battle.' Then when they urgently asked him what had happened and desired to know, he said evasively: 'Oh, my sons, look at the sky, consider how wonderful it is, and think how inscrutable are the judgments of God' and so forth. And so after a few days they learned that it had been announced far and wide that a wretched and mournful battle had taken place at

the very day and hour in which it had been revealed to him.

Concerning the hermit who died in that hour which the
holy bishop had prophesied for his own decease

At the above-mentioned city of Carlisle there was
a certain worthy anchorite named Hereberht from
the islands of a western lake. He had constantly on
previous occasions made his way to the bishop and
now again sought to have converse with him.
According to his custom, he sought spiritual converse and renewed their frequent prayers together.
And the holy bishop, after many spiritual words
whereby he gave him instruction, said prophetically
to him, as he had told many: 'O beloved brother,
speak and ask what things are necessary for you, for
from this hour, as St Paul declared to the Ephe-
sians, we shall never again see each other in this
world.'

Then the anchorite, falling on his knees at his
feet, with lamentation and tears said: 'I adjure you
by Jesus Christ, the Son of God, that you ask the
Holy Trinity not to leave me in this present world
bereaved of you after your death, but that He may
receive me with you into the joy of the eternal
kingdom.' Cuthbert immediately prayed to Him
and then answered him as he lay there: 'Rise and
rejoice, for your request has been obtained for you

by the Lord Jesus Christ according to your words
and you will undoubtedly receive it.'

Why should I delay by making a long story of
this? At the same time, in the same night, and at
the same hour of the night, the bishop and the
anchorite both died according to the bishop's
promise, and they reign together with Christ for
ever and ever.

How he saw the soul of a brother, who fell from a tree,
being carried to heaven

The most faithful abbess Aelflaed related to me
another miracle of spiritual knowledge concerning
the holy bishop. For when on a certain day, she
was sitting feasting with him at a place in his
diocese called Ovington she saw the man of God
in a trance and seized with ecstasy; and the knife
which he had in his hand dropped and fell on to
the table. Then unheard by the others, she humbly
asked him what it was that had been revealed to
him. He answered: 'I saw the soul of a servant of
God from your household being carried to heaven
in the hands of angels and being set amid the choir
of angels, saints, and martyrs.'

When she asked his name he replied: 'You will
name him to me tomorrow when I am celebrating
Mass!' And that same hour the abbess sent a messenger to her monastery to ask which of the breth-

ren had lately died, but he found them all alive there. Finally, after diligent enquiries, they heard that one of the brethren in the shepherds' huts had fallen down from the top of a tree and was dead, all his bones being broken. Now the messenger on the next day returned to the abbess and told her what had happened. She immediately ran in to the holy bishop, who was dedicating a church there on that day and, as they were singing Mass, at the place where it says, 'Remember, Lord, thy servants,' she came breathless into the church and declared the name of the brother, who was called Hadwald, realizing not only that in this matter there was in him a spirit of prophecy, but also perceiving in all things his apostolic foresight whereby he also clearly foretold his own death in many ways.

How, of his own accord, he returned from his bishopric to his former mode of life

So after two years he resigned of his own will the worldly honours of his bishopric, for being filled with the prophetic spirit of God, he foresaw his death and, being attracted by the love of his former solitary way of life, he returned to the island from which he had formerly been withdrawn by compulsion. So he remained alone, satisfied with the converse and ministry of angels, full of hope and putting his trust wholly in God, though his body was now infirm and afflicted with a certain sickness.

Concerning the one who was healed of dysentery

And so during the last period of his illness, he ordered a certain faithful well-tried brother, still surviving and called Walhstod, who at that time suffered from dysentery, to come specially to minister to him in his cell. He gladly consented and at the saint's first touch, as he frequently narrated, recalling the story with tears, the grievous sickness entirely deserted him, and though afflicted before and, as it were, given up to death, he felt himself to be restored to life and health, and thankfully informed the brethren.

How he departed to be with the Lord without a struggle and was honourably buried in our church

But after Bishop Cuthbert of holy memory had taken communion and lifted up his eyes and hands to heaven, he commended his soul to the Lord, and, sitting there, he breathed his last, and without a sigh went in the way of his fathers. He was carried by ship to our island; but first his whole body was washed, his head wrapped in a head cloth and an obley placed upon his holy breast. He was robed in his priestly garments, wearing his shoes in readiness to meet Christ and provided with a waxed shroud. His soul rejoicing in Christ, his body remained incorrupt, resting as though asleep in his stone coffin; and so they placed him with honour in the church.

The Synod of Whitby

Bede, *Ecclesiastical History*, Book III, Chapter 25

A dispute arises with those who came from Ireland concerning the date of Easter

Meanwhile, after Bishop Aidan had departed this life Finan had succeeded him as bishop, having been consecrated and sent by the Irish. On the island of Lindisfarne he built a church befitting an episcopal see, although he constructed it in the Irish manner entirely of hewn oak, not of stone, and thatched it with reeds; and it was later consecrated by the most reverend Archbishop Theodore to the honour of the blessed apostle Peter. However, Bishop Eadbert of Lindisfarne had the thatch removed and the whole church, that is to say not only the roof but the walls as well, covered with sheets of lead.

At this time there arose serious and recurrent controversy about the date of Easter. Those who had come from Kent and Gaul declared that the Irish observance of Easter Sunday was contrary to the practice of the universal Church. One particu-

larly vigorous champion of the true Easter, named
Ronan, was Irish by race but had been instructed
in the authentic practice of the Church in Gaul or
Italy. In his dispute with Finan he convinced many
people, or at least spurred them to a more careful
investigation of the truth, but he had no success at
all in correcting Finan; on the contrary, being a
man of headstrong temperament he made him
embittered by his criticisms and turned him into an
open opponent of the truth. James, once deacon of
the venerable Archbishop Paulinus, observed the
true, Catholic Easter along with all those that he
could instruct in the better way. Queen Eanfled,
too, and her court, who had with her a priest from
Kent named Romanus who followed the Catholic
practice, observed Easter according to the tradition
she had seen in Kent. As a consequence, it is said
to have often come about in those days that Easter
was celebrated twice in a single year, with the
queen and her court still observing Lent and
celebrating Palm Sunday at the very same time as
the king had finished the fast and was keeping
Easter Sunday. During the lifetime of Aidan, this
disagreement about the keeping of Easter was
borne with patience by everyone, because they
knew full well that although he could not keep
Easter otherwise than according to the practice of
those who had sent him, nevertheless those works
of faith, piety and love that he set himself diligently

to perform were true to the practice of all the saints. He was therefore deservedly loved by everyone, even those who held different opinions about Easter; and not only ordinary people but bishops, too, like Honorius of Canterbury and Felix of East Anglia, held him in reverence.

After the death of his successor Finan, another Irishman, Colman, became bishop, and a serious controversy arose not only about the observance of Easter but about other matters of church discipline. This dispute naturally troubled the minds and hearts of many people, who were afraid that after taking the name of Christian they were running or had run in vain. It came to the ears of the rulers themselves, King Oswy and his son Alchfrith. Oswy, who had been taught and baptized by the Irish and was also well versed in their language, believed that nothing could be better than their teaching; whereas Alchfrith had been taught the Christian faith by Wilfrid, a man of great learning, and knew that his teaching was really to be preferred to all the traditions of the Irish. For Wilfrid had once been to Rome to study the doctrine of the Church, and had spent a long time at Lugdunum with Dalfinus, archbishop of Gaul, from whom he had received the Church's tonsure in the form of a crown. It was for this reason that Alchfrith had given him a monastery with forty hides of land at a place named In Hrypum. This was a site

that he had given for a monastery a little earlier to
the followers of Irish ways; but afterwards, when
given a choice, they preferred to leave the place
rather than change their practices, and he gave it to
a man worthy of it by his teaching as well as his
way of life. At that time Agilbert, bishop of the
West Saxons, whom we have mentioned above, a
friend of King Alchfrith and Abbot Wilfrid, had
arrived in Northumbria, and spent some time
there. At the request of Alchfrith he ordained
Wilfrid priest in his own monastery. With him he
had a priest called Agatho.

In consequence of the dispute that had arisen in
Northumbria about Easter, and the tonsure, and
other Church matters, it was arranged that a council should be held to settle the dispute in the
monastery called Streanaeshalch, meaning bay of
the lighthouse, whose abbess was at that time Hild,
a woman devoted to God. It was attended by both
kings, father and son; Bishop Colman with his
clergy from Ireland; and Bishop Agilbert with the
priests Agatho and Wilfrid. James and Romanus
were on their side — while Abbess Hild and her
followers were on the side of the Irish, which
included the venerable Bishop Cedd; he had been
ordained by the Irish long before and acted at that
council as a most scrupulous interpreter for both
sides.

King Oswy opened the discussion by saying that

those who served one God ought to have one rule of life and not differ in the celebration of the heavenly sacraments, since they all hoped for one kingdom in Heaven; they ought rather to inquire which was the truer tradition, and all follow it together. He then told his bishop Colman to speak first and explain the usage that he followed, and its origin. Colman then said: 'This method of keeping Easter which I observe, I received from my superiors, who sent me here as bishop; and all our fathers, men beloved of God, are known to have followed the same observance. In case any should judge it a matter for contempt and reproach, it is recorded that this very same observance was followed by the blessed evangelist John, a disciple specially dear to the Lord, and by all the churches over which he presided.'

After Colman had spoken along these lines, the king told Agilbert to declare his method of observance, together with its origin and the authority he had for following it. Agilbert replied: 'I request that my disciple, the priest Wilfrid, may speak instead of me, as we are both of the same mind as the other followers of the Church's tradition who are seated here, and he can give a better and clearer explanation of our view in the English language than I can through an interpreter.'

Then Wilfrid was bidden to speak by the king, and began thus: 'The Easter that we observe is the one we saw celebrated by everyone at Rome, where the blessed apostles Peter and Paul lived, taught, suffered and were buried. It is a usage we found to be universal in Italy and in Gaul, lands that we have travelled over for the purpose of study and prayer. In Africa, Asia, Egypt, Greece, and every part of the world, where the Church of Christ is scattered, we learned that this practice is followed by different nations speaking different languages, and all at one and the same time. The only exceptions are this people and their accomplices in stubbornness, I mean the Picts and the Britons, who from these two remotest islands in the Ocean, and from only parts of them, pursue a foolish struggle against the whole world.'

To these words of his Colman replied: 'I find it remarkable that you choose to call our struggle foolish, when we follow the example of that great apostle who was worthy to recline upon his Lord's breast, and who, as all the world knows, lived a life of great wisdom.'

Wilfrid answered: 'Far be it from us to reproach John with foolishness. He observed to the letter the decrees of the Law of Moses at a time when the Church still followed Jewish practice in many matters. The apostles were not able to abolish at a stroke the entire observance of the Law ordained by God, in the same way as there is an obligation on all who come to the faith to renounce idols invented by devils. They were afraid to create a stumbling-block for those Jews who were dispersed among the gentiles. It was for this reason that Paul circumcized Timothy, that he sacrificed victims in the temple, and that with Aquila and Priscilla he shaved his head at Corinth; the only purpose being to avoid scandalizing the Jews. It was for this reason that James said to Paul: "Thou seest, brother, how many thousands there are among the Jews of them which have believed; and they are all zealous for the Law."

'Yet today, now that the Gospel shines brightly through the world, it is not necessary, or even lawful, for the faithful to be circumcized or to offer God sacrifices of flesh and blood. John, therefore, began the celebration of Easter according to the practice of the Law, in the evening of the fourteenth day of the first month, regardless of whether it fell on the Sabbath or any other day. But when Peter was preaching at Rome, remembering that the Lord rose from the dead, and brought to the world the hope of resurrection, on the day after the Sabbath, he realized that Easter should be kept according to the following rule: following the custom and precepts of the Law, he always waited for the rising of the moon in the evening of the fourteenth day of the first month, just as John did; if the Lord's Day, which was then called the first after the Sabbath, was to fall on the morning after the moon's rising, he began to celebrate Easter on that evening, as we all do today; but if the Lord's Day was not due on the morning after the fourteenth day of the moon, but on the sixteenth or seventeenth or any other day up to the twenty-first, he waited for it, and began the solemn rites of Easter the night before, on the evening of the Sabbath, so that Easter Sunday was always kept between the fifteenth and the twenty-first day of the moon.

'This evangelical and apostolical tradition does not abrogate, but rather is the fulfilment of, the Law, in which it is decreed that the Passover should be observed between the evening of the fourteenth day of the moon in the first month and the evening of the twenty-first day of the moon in the same month. All the successors of blessed John in Asia since his death, and the whole Church throughout the world, have come to follow this observance. That this is the true Easter, and the only one to be celebrated by the faithful, was reaffirmed, and not newly decided, by the Council of Nicaea, as the history of the Church teaches us.

'From this evidence it is clear, Colman, that you follow neither the example of John, as you suppose, nor that of Peter, whose tradition you knowingly contradict, and that your observance of Easter accords with neither the Law nor the Gospel. For John, who kept Easter according to the decrees of the Law of Moses, attached no importance to the first day after the Sabbath; you differ from him in that you always celebrate Easter on the first day after the Sabbath. Peter celebrated Easter Sunday between the fifteenth and the twenty-first day of the moon; you, on the other hand, keep Easter Sunday between the fourteenth and the twentieth day of the moon, and often begin Easter in the evening of the thirteenth day. The Law makes no mention of this, and it was not on this day but on the fourteenth that the Lord who is the author and giver of the Gospel ate the old Passover in the evening, and instituted the sacraments of the New Testament for the Church to celebrate in commemoration of His passion. Again, the twenty-first day of the moon, which the Law particularly ordered to be observed, is completely excluded by your observance of Easter. So, as I have said, in your celebration of the greatest of festivals you agree neither with John, nor with Peter, nor with the Law, nor with the Gospel.'

Colman's reply was as follows: 'Did Anatolius, a holy man who was highly praised in that history of the Church that you refer to, and who wrote that Easter should be celebrated between the fourteenth and twentieth days of the moon, hold a belief contrary to the Law and the Gospel? Are we to believe that our most reverend father Columba and his successors, men beloved of God, who kept

Easter in the same way, believed and acted contrary to the holy scriptures? There were many among them to whose holiness signs from Heaven and the miracles which they performed bore testimony. I have no doubt that they were saints, and I never cease to follow their way of life, their customs and their teaching.'

Wilfrid answered: 'We all agree that Anatolius was a most holy and learned man and worthy of the highest praise; but what have you to do with him, seeing that you fail even to follow his instructions? In his observance of Easter he followed a correct rule and established a cycle of nineteen years, which you are either unaware of or treat with contempt, though it is recognized and observed by the whole Church of Christ. He assigned the fourteenth day of the moon to Easter Sunday because he reckoned in the Egyptian manner and counted the evening of the fourteenth as the start of the fifteenth day. In the same way in assigning the twentieth day to Easter Sunday he included its latter part in the twenty-first. That you are ignorant of this distinction is proved by the fact that you sometimes quite clearly keep Easter before the full moon, that is on the thirteenth day of the moon.

'As regards your father Columba and his followers, whose holiness you claim to imitate and whose rule and teaching confirmed by signs from Heaven you claim to follow, I might reply that on the Day of Judgement there will be many saying to the Lord that they prophesied in His name, and cast out devils, and performed many miracles: but the Lord will reply that He never knew them. But far be it from me to say this about your fathers: it is much better to believe good than evil of those of whom nothing is known. So I will not deny that they were God's servants and beloved of God, who loved God in simple ignorance and pious intent. Nor do I think that their observance of Easter did them much harm, as long as no one had come to show them a more accurate tradition to follow; indeed, I believe that if any observer of the Catholic rule had come to them they would have fol- . lowed his guidance, just as we know they followed all those of God's laws that came to their knowledge. You, however, and your supporters have heard the decrees of the Apostolic See, or rather of the universal Church, which are confirmed by the holy scriptures; and if you disdain to follow them there can be no doubt of your guilt. Your fathers may have been holy men, yet are they, a few men in one corner of a remote island, to have precedence over the universal Church of Christ throughout the world? Your father Columba, and ours, too, if he belonged to Christ, may have had miraculous powers, yet could he have precedence over the most blessed chief of the apostles, to whom the Lord said: "Thou art Peter, and upon this rock I will build my Church, and the gates of Hell shall not prevail against it, and I will give unto thee the keys of the Kingdom of Heaven"?'

After these closing words from Wilfrid, the king said: 'Is it true, Colman, that these words were spoken to Peter by the Lord?' Colman said: 'It is true, Your Majesty.'

The king asked: 'Can you produce any evidence that similar authority was given to your father Columba?' He answered: 'None.' The king went on: 'Do you both agree without any question that these words were addressed chiefly to Peter, and that it was to him that the keys of the Kingdom of Heaven were given by the Lord?' They both answered: 'Yes.'

The king concluded as follows: 'Then I tell you that he is that keeper of the gate, and I will not contradict him. To the best of my knowledge and powers I desire to obey his commands in everything, in case when I come to the gates of the Kingdom of Heaven he, who by your testimony holds the keys, should turn away, and there be no one to open for me.'

When the king had spoken, all those who sat or stood there, both high and low, expressed their agreement; and they gave up their inaccurate observance and were quick to adopt what they now knew to be the better rule.

Bede, *Ecclesiastical History*, Book III, Chapter 26

*After his defeat Colman returns home, and Tuda
becomes bishop in his place; the state of the church
under these teachers*

When the dispute had been ended and the assembly dissolved, Agilbert returned home. Seeing his teaching rejected and his principles discounted, Colman took those who wished to follow him and refused to accept the Catholic Easter and the tonsure in the form of a crown, about which there had also been much discussion, and went back to the Irish to discuss with his people what action to take about it. Cedd returned to his bishopric and abandoned Irish practices, accepting the Catholic observation of Easter. This debate occurred in the year of our Lord 664, which was the twenty-second year of Oswy's reign, and the thirtieth year of the Irish episcopate in England, as Aidan was bishop for seventeen years, Finan for ten, and Colman for three.

When Colman returned home he was succeeded as bishop of Northumbria by Christ's servant Tuda, who had been educated and consecrated bishop among the southern Irish and who, in accordance with the custom of that kingdom, had the ecclesiastical tonsure in the form of a crown and observed the Catholic rule for the time of Easter. He was a good and devout man but governed the Church for only a very short time. He had come from Ireland during Colman's episcopate, and was diligent in teaching all men, by his word and his example, the doctrines of the true faith. The brothers who preferred to stay in the church of Lindisfarne when the Irish departed were put under the charge of a new abbot, Eata, a most reverend and kindly man who was abbot of the monastery of Mailros. This is said to have been done by King Oswy at the special request of Colman before his departure, as Eata was one of twelve boys of English race whom Aidan took at the start of his episcopate to give a Christian education; and the king had great love for Bishop Colman because of his innate good sense. Eata was the same man who a little later became bishop of the church of Lindisfarne. Colman on his departure for home took with him some of the bones of the most reverend father Aidan, leaving the remainder in the church of which he had charge with the instruction that they be buried in its sanctuary.

Evidence of the great frugality and austerity practised by Colman and his predecessors was afforded by the place over which they ruled, for on their departure only a very few buildings were found there, apart from the church, consisting only of those necessary to any civilized community. They owned no wealth apart from their livestock, since any money they received from the rich was at once given to the poor. They had no need to save money or provide accommodation in order to receive the rulers of the world, who only came to the church for the purpose of prayer and to hear the word of God. The king himself, whenever the opportunity allowed it, came with only five or six thanes, and went away after completing his prayers in the church. Even if it chanced that they had a meal there they were content with the simple daily fare of the brothers, and asked for nothing more. The sole concern of the teachers of those days was to serve God, not the world, and to feed the soul, not the belly. The religious habit, therefore, was held in great respect at that time, so that whenever a cleric or monk appeared he was welcomed gladly by everyone as a servant of God. Even if one was discovered passing on the road, they would run up to him and bow their heads, and were glad to be signed with the cross by his hand or blessed by his lips; and they paid close heed to such men's exhortations. On the Lord's Day they gathered eagerly in the church or the monasteries, not to get food for their bodies but to listen to the word of God; and if a priest came by chance to their village the people at once came together, eager to receive from him the word of life. The priests and clerics themselves visited their villages for no other reason than to preach, baptize, visit the sick and, in sum, to care for their souls; and so free were they from any taint of avarice that none accepted grants of land and estates for building monasteries unless compelled by the secular rulers. For some time afterwards this continued to be the practice of all the churches in Northumbria. But enough has now been said on these matters.

Eddius Stephanus, Chapter X

Of the strife of St Wilfrid the priest with Bishop Colman about the keeping of Easter

On a certain occasion in the days of Colman, Bishop of York and Metropolitan, while Oswy and Alchfrith his son were reigning, the abbots and priests and men of all ranks in the orders of the Church gathered together in a monastery called Whitby, in the presence of the holy mother and most pious nun Hild, as well as of the kings and two bishops, namely Colman and Agilbert, to consider the question of the proper date for the keeping of Easter whether in accordance with the British and Scottish manner and that of the whole of the northern district, Easter should be kept on the Sunday between the fourteenth day of the moon and the twenty-second, or whether the plan of the Apostolic See was better, namely to celebrate

Easter Sunday between the fifteenth day of the moon and the twenty-first. The opportunity was granted first of all to Bishop Colman, as was proper, to state his case in the presence of all. He boldly spoke in reply as follows: 'Our fathers and their predecessors, plainly inspired by the Holy Spirit as was Columba, ordained the celebration of Easter on the fourteenth day of the moon, if it was a Sunday, following the example of the Apostle and Evangelist John "who leaned on the breast of the Lord at supper" and was called the friend of the Lord. He celebrated Easter on the fourteenth day of the moon and we, like his disciples Polycarp and others, celebrate it on his authority; we dare not change it, for our fathers' sake, nor do we wish to do so. I have expressed the opinion of our party, do you state yours.'

Agilbert the foreign bishop and Agatho his priest bade St Wilfrid, priest and abbot, with his persuasive eloquence explain in his own tongue the system of the Roman Church and of the Apostolic See. With his customary humility he answered in these words:

'This question has already been admirably investigated by the three hundred and eighteen most holy and learned fathers gathered together in Nicaea, a city of Bithynia. They fixed amongst other decisions upon a lunar cycle which recurs every nineteen years. This cycle never shows that

Easter is to be kept on the fourteenth day of the moon. This is the fixed rule of the Apostolic See and of almost the whole world and our fathers, after many decrees had been made, uttered these words: "he who condemns any one of these let him be accursed." '

Then, after St Wilfrid the priest had finished his speech, King Oswy smilingly asked them all, 'Tell me which is greater in the Kingdom of Heaven, Columba or the Apostle Peter?' The whole synod answered with one voice and one consent, 'The Lord settled this when He declared: "Thou art Peter and upon this rock I will build my Church and the gates of Hell shall not prevail against it. And I will give thee the keys of the Kingdom of Heaven; and whatsoever thou shalt bind on earth shall be bound in Heaven; and whatsoever thou shalt loose on earth shall be loosed in Heaven." '

The king wisely replied, 'He is the porter and keeps the keys. With him I will have no differences nor will I agree with those who have such, nor in any single particular will I gainsay his decisions so long as I live.'

So Bishop Colman was told what he must do, should he reject the tonsure and the Easter rule for fear of his fellow-countrymen, namely, he must retire and leave his see to be taken by another and a better man. Thus indeed he did.

Bede, *Ecclesiastical History,* Book IV, Chapter 4

After leaving Britain, Bishop Colman founds two
monasteries in Ireland

Meanwhile Colman, who was a bishop from
Ireland, left Britain and took with him all the Irish
whom he had gathered on the island of Lindisfarne;
and also about thirty men of English race, both
groups being thoroughly instructed in the monastic
way of life. Leaving some brothers in his church,
he went first to the island of Hii, from where he
had been appointed to preach the word to the
English. He then withdrew to a small and remote
island off the west coast of Ireland, called Inis-
boufind, meaning the island of the white heifer.
On his arrival there he built a monastery and
housed in it the monks whom he had assembled
from both races and brought with him. They were
unable to live in harmony with each other, as in
summertime, when the harvest had to be gathered,
the Irish left the monastery and strayed in different
directions over the country which was familiar to
them; yet they returned on the approach of winter,
expecting to share in the supplies provided by the
English. Colman, therefore, looked for a means of
healing the dispute, and after searching everywhere
far and near he found a place suitable for building

a monastery on the Irish mainland, called in the Irish language Mag éo. He bought a small part of it to build a monastery on from the nobleman to whose estate it belonged, on condition that the monks who settled there should offer prayers to the Lord for the provider of the land. The monastery was built at once with the help of the nobleman and all his neighbours, and Colman housed the English there, leaving the Irish on the island. This monastery is still occupied by Englishmen. From its modest beginning it has grown today into a large monastery, usually called Muig éo, and its entire community were converted long ago to better practices. It has an excellent company of monks, gathered there from England, who live after the example of the venerable fathers under a Rule and a canonically elected abbot, in strict and devout self-denial and by the labour of their own hands.

St Chad

Eddius Stephanus, Chapter XV

How St Chad was restored to his see

So, after the lapse of three years, Archbishop Theodore came from Kent to the King of Deira and Bernicia, bringing with him the decrees of the Apostolic See from which he had been sent. As soon as he had reached that land he heard from the lips of true witnesses the story of the offence against the canon law and how one bishop had dared, like a thief, to snatch another bishop's see. He indignantly ordered that Bishop Chad should be deposed from the see of another man.

Chad, being a true and meek servant of God and fully understanding then the wrongdoing implied in his ordination to another's see by the Quartodecimans, with humble penance confessed his fault in accordance with the decision of the bishops: whereupon Theodore, with Chad's consent, installed St Wilfrid as bishop in his own see of York. Then our holy bishop, in accordance with the command of the Lord, returned good for evil, not evil for evil, just as David did to Saul when he said, 'I will not stretch forth my hand against the Lord's anointed.' He knew of a place in the kingdom of Wulfhere, King of the Mercians, his faithful friend, which had been granted to him at Lichfield and was suitable as an episcopal see either for himself or for any other to whom he might wish to give it. So a friendly arrangement was made with that true servant of God, Chad, who in all things obeyed the bishops: they thereupon consecrated him fully to the said see through all the ecclesiastical degrees. The king received him in an honourable manner and the bishops installed him in the said place. There he performed many good and pious deeds during his life, and at the fitting time he passed to his fathers, awaiting the day when the Lord shall come in judgment, a day which we believe will rightly have no terrors for him.

St Hilda

Bede, *Ecclesiastical History*, Book IV, Chapter 23

The life and death of Abbess Hild

In the following year, the year of our Lord 680, Christ's most devout servant Hild, the abbess of the monastery called Streanaeshalch, as previously mentioned, was taken from this earth on the seventeenth day of November, to enjoy the reward of heavenly life after all the works of Heaven that she performed on earth. She lived for sixty-six years, and her life fell into two equal parts: for the first thirty-three years she spent a noble life in the secular habit, while the second half she dedicated yet more nobly to the Lord in the monastic life. For she was of noble birth, daughter of King Edwin's nephew Hereric, and in company with Edwin she received the faith and mysteries of Christ during the mission of Paulinus of blessed memory, the first bishop of the Northumbrians; and she preserved that faith inviolate until judged worthy to see Him face to face.

After resolving to retire from secular life and serve Him alone, she withdrew to the kingdom of the East Angles to whose king she was related. She wished if possible to leave her home and all her possessions and cross over to Gaul, where she intended to live as an exile for the Lord's sake in the monastery of Cale, the more easily to earn an everlasting home in Heaven. In the same monastery at that time her sister Hereswith, mother of Aldwulf the king of the East Angles, was living by the monastic Rule and awaiting her eternal crown; and inspired by her example Hild remained in that kingdom a whole year intending to travel abroad. However, she was then summoned home by Bishop Aidan and given land one hide in area to the north of the river Wear, where she lived the monastic life for a further year with a small number of companions.

After this she became abbess of the monastery of Heruteu, founded a little earlier by Christ's devout servant Heiu, who is said to have been the first woman in the kingdom of the Northumbrians to take the vows and habit of the religious life, when she was ordained by Bishop Aidan. Not long after the monastery's foundation Heiu left for the city of Calcaria, which the English call Kaelcacaestir, and made her home there; and Christ's servant Hild was appointed to take charge of the monastery. She at once set about ordering all its life according to a

Rule, following the guidance of learned men; for Bishop Aidan and other devout men who knew her, in recognition of her innate wisdom and devotion to God's service, used to visit her frequently in heartfelt affection and give her careful instruction.

After having charge of this monastery for some years, preoccupied with maintaining the life of the Rule, she was appointed also to found or set in order a monastery at a place called Streanaeshalch, and carried out her task with energy. She established the discipline of the same monastic Rule as in her previous monastery, and there too she taught the strict observance of justice, holiness and chastity and all the virtues, but especially peace and charity; and in imitation of the early Church there was no one rich or in need there, for they held all things in common and nothing was regarded as anyone's private possession. Such was her own good sense that her advice was sought and obtained not only by ordinary folk in difficulties but often too by kings and rulers. She required those under her to devote so much time to reading the holy scriptures and to the practice of good works that there were many in that community found fit to enter holy orders and the service of the altar.

For example, we have seen five members of that monastery go on to become bishops, all of them men of exceptional worth and holiness; their names

are Bosa, Aetla, Oftfor, John and Wilfrid. Of the
first of these we have mentioned earlier that he was
consecrated bishop of Eboracum; of the second we
must briefly remark that he was consecrated bishop
of Dorciccaestra; and of the last two, consecrated
respectively bishop of Hagustaldesea and bishop of
Eboracum, we must speak below. Of Oftfor we
may say at this point that he devoted himself to the
reading and observance of the scriptures in both of
Abbess Hild's monasteries, but at length in search
of still greater perfection went to Kent to Archbishop Theodore of blessed memory. After spending some time there in the study of sacred texts he
also undertook the journey to Rome, which at that
time was regarded as especially meritorious. Returning from Rome to Britain, he visited the
kingdom of the Hwiccas, then ruled by King
Osric, and stayed there a long time preaching the
word of the faith and setting an example of holy
living to those who saw and heard him. At the
time the bishop of that kingdom, whose name was
Bosel, was so burdened by ill health that he could
not fulfil his episcopal duties himself, and so by
general consent Oftfor was chosen bishop in his
place and at the bidding of King Aethelred consecrated by Bishop Wilfrid of blessed memory.
Wilfrid at that time was acting as bishop of the
Middle Angles, as Archbishop Theodore had died
and no one had yet been appointed bishop to

succeed him. Shortly before God's servant Bosel
became bishop, Tatfrith, a man of great energy and
learning and of outstanding ability, was chosen to
be bishop of that kingdom, and he also was from
Abbess Hild's monastery; but before he could be
consecrated his life was cut short by an untimely
death.

Abbess Hild, then, the handmaid of Christ, who
was called mother by all who knew her for her
exceptional devotion and grace, not only set a
pattern of life for the community in her own
monastery but also enabled many who lived further
afield, and who had heard the happy report of her
industry and virtue, to obtain salvation and repen-
tance. This was in fulfilment of a dream which her
mother Breguswith had when Hild was in her
infancy. While her husband Hereric was in exile
under the king of the Britons, Cerdic, where he
later died by poison, she had a dream in which he
was suddenly taken from her, and though she
searched for him with the utmost care no trace of
him could be found anywhere. However, after
searching thoroughly she suddenly found under her
dress a most precious necklace; and as she exam-
ined it more closely it seemed to shine with such
a blaze of light that it filled all the land of Britain
with the beauty of its radiance. There is no doubt
that this dream was fulfilled in her daughter, of
whom we are speaking, since her life afforded

examples of the works of light not only for herself but for many others who wished to lead a good life.

After she had been in charge of this monastery for many years, it pleased the merciful Author of our salvation that her holy soul be tested by a long infirmity of the body in order that, following the example of the apostle, her strength might be made perfect in weakness. She was afflicted with a fever that exhausted her with its burning heat, and for six years continuously she suffered from it without respite; yet in all that time she never ceased to give thanks to her Maker or to teach, in public and in private, the flock entrusted to her. Taught by her own example, she warned them all that when in bodily health they should serve the Lord in obedience, and when in adversity or sickness always give thanks to the Lord in faithfulness. In the seventh year of her sickness she had begun to suffer internal pain, and came to her last day. About cock-crow she received the viaticum of the holy communion, and then summoned the handmaids of Christ who were in the monastery to urge them to keep the peace of the Gospel with each other, and indeed with all the world; and while she was exhorting them she joyfully met her death, or rather, in the words of the Lord, she passed from death to life.

That same night it pleased Almighty God to

make known her death by a vision in another monastery some distance away, called Hacanos, which she had built the same year. In this monastery there was a nun named Begu, who for more than thirty years had been vowed to chastity and served the Lord in the monastic life. On this occasion she was resting in the sisters' dormitory when she suddenly heard in the air the familiar sound of the bell which used to rouse them for prayers and call them together when one of them had been summoned from the world. Opening her eyes, as she thought, she saw that the roof of the house had been removed and all was filled with light flooding down from above; and while gazing intently into this light she saw, in the light itself, the soul of God's servant Hild, escorted by a company of angels, being borne to Heaven. Waking from her sleep she saw the other sisters resting round about her, and realized that what she had seen had been revealed to her in a dream or a vision. Rising at once in great terror she ran to the sister who was in charge of the monastery at the time in place of the abbess, and whose name was Frigyth, and with streams of tears and deep sighs of regret announced that the mother of them all, Abbess Hild, had now departed from the world, and while she watched, in the midst of a great light and escorted by angels, had ascended to the abode of eternal light to join the citizens of Heaven.

When Frigyth heard this, she roused all the sisters, summoned them to the church, and ordered them to pray and sing psalms for the soul of their mother. They did this assiduously for the remainder of the night, and at first light there arrived brothers from the place where she died, to announce her death. They replied that they already knew of it, and when they explained in detail how and when they had learned the news it was found that her death had been revealed to them in a vision at the same hour as the brothers reported that she had departed from the world. So by a beautiful conjunction of events God brought it about that while some witnessed her departure from this life, others at the same time watched her entry into the everlasting life of the spirit. These monasteries, moreover, are almost thirteen miles apart.

They also say that on the same night, and in the same monastery where God's servant died, her death was revealed in a vision to one of the virgins dedicated to God, who had an especial love for her. She saw her soul going to Heaven with the angels, and at the very hour when it occurred gave a clear account to the servants of Christ who were with her, and roused them to pray for her soul even before the rest of the community learned of her death. It was early next morning when the others assembled and were told what had happened, as this nun was at the time living separately with some others in the furthest part of the monastery, where women who had recently entered the monastic life used to serve their probation until they were instructed in the Rule and admitted into the fellowship of the community.

St Bede

Ecclesiastical History, Book V, Chapter 24

My own life

With the Lord's help, I, Bede, a servant of Christ
and priest of the monastery of the blessed apostles
Peter and Paul at Wiuraemuda and In Gyrwum,
have composed this Ecclesiastical History of Britain,
and of the English people in particular, using whatever information I could acquire from ancient
documents, from the tradition of my elders, and
from my own knowledge. I was born on the lands
of this monastery, and at the age of seven was
entrusted by the care of my family to the reverend
Abbot Benedict, and then to Ceolfrith, to be
educated. Since then I have lived my whole life in
this monastery, devoting myself entirely to the
study of the scriptures; and amid the observance of
the discipline of the Rule and the daily task of
singing in the church, it has always been my
delight to learn, to teach or to write. I was ordained deacon at the age of nineteen and priest at
the age of thirty, on both occasions through the

ministration of the reverend Bishop John and at the bidding of Abbot Ceolfrith. From the time of my entering the priesthood until my fifty-ninth year, I have made it my business, for my own and my brothers' use, to compile brief notes on the holy scriptures extracted from the works of the venerable fathers, and to make additional comments to clarify their meaning and interpretation.

The Death of St Bede

Bishop Cuthbert's Letter to Lul

To his most beloved fellow-teacher in Christ Cuthwin, Cuthbert his fellow-disciple wishes eternal salvation in God. The little present which you sent me I received with much gratitude, and with much pleasure I read your devoutly learned letter; from these I found out what I specially desired to know, that you are lovingly offering Masses and fervent prayers for our father and master Bede, beloved of God.

Therefore, through love of him rather than through confidence in my own ability, I am delighted to tell you in these few words how he passed from this world, since I understand that this is what you desired, this is what you requested.

He was indeed troubled by illness and especially frequent breathlessness, yet he was almost without pain before the day of the Lord's Resurrection, that is for almost two weeks; after Easter he continued in the same state, cheerful and joyful, and giving thanks to Almighty God every day and every night and indeed every hour until the day of the Lord's Ascension, which was the 26th of May.

Every day he gave lessons to us, his students; for the rest of   the day he was busy singing the psalms as best he could. He would spend the whole night in prayer and thanksgiving to God unless a short sleep prevented him. When he woke again, he immediately meditated on the accustomed chants from Scripture, not forgetting to give thanks to God with hands outstretched.

In all truth I can say that I never saw nor heard any other man so diligent in giving thanks to the living God. 'O truly blessed man.' He often sang the sentence of St Paul the Apostle, saying: 'It is a fearful thing to fall into the hands of the living God' as well as many other words of Scripture, with which he admonished us from the slumber of the soul by thinking in good time about our last hours. And in our own language (as he knew our poems well) he would say:

> Before that enforced journey no one becomes
> Wiser in thought than he may need be,
> For considering before his going hence
> What for his spirit of good or evil
> After his death day might be judged.

He would also sing antiphons for our consolation and his, of which this is one:

O king of glory, lord of Might,
Who rose today in victory above all the
    heavens,
Do not leave us orphans,
But send us the Father's promised Spirit of
    Truth,
Alleluia.

When he came to the words 'Do not leave us orphans', he burst into tears and wept copiously. After an hour he would repeat what he had left unfinished and thus he continued the whole day. And when we heard this, we shared his sorrow and wept; we wept and cried in turn; indeed we wept as we studied. In this kind of joy we passed Paschaltide until the same Ascension Day.

And he rejoiced exceedingly and gave God thanks because he had deserved to suffer in this way, and he would often say: 'God chastises every son whom he receives' as well as the words of Ambrose: 'I have not lived in such a way that I am ashamed to continue life among you, but I do not fear to die, because we have a uniquely good God.'

In these days, besides our lessons and the chanting of psalms he was much busied with two short works which are specially worthy of memory: the translation into our own language for the Church's benefit of the Gospel of St John from the beginning until the passage where it says: 'But what are these among so many?' and also certain excerpts from the Book of Cycles by Bishop Isidore, about which he said: 'I do not wish my students to read lies, or to work at this task in vain after my death.'

When the Tuesday before the Lord's Ascension came, his breathing became much worse and a small swelling appeared in his feet.

Nonetheless he continued his teaching all that day and dictated cheerfully; among other things he said several times: 'Learn quickly now, for I do not know how long I shall live, nor whether after a short time my Maker will take me.' But he seemed to us to know very well when his end would come. And so he spent all that night awake in thanksgiving.

At daybreak on Wednesday he told us to finish the writing which we had begun. We did this until the third hour. From then onwards we processed with the relics of the saints, as the custom of that day required.

There was one of us with him who said: 'Beloved master, there is still one chapter missing from the book you were dictating, but it seems to me difficult to ask you for more.' But he answered: 'It is easy. Take your pen and prepare it and write quickly.' And this he did.

At the ninth hour he said to me: 'I have a few treasures in my little box: pepper, handkerchiefs and incense. Run quickly and fetch the priests of our monastery to me, so that I can distribute to them these little gifts which God has given me.'

This I did with some trembling. When they came he spoke to them, urgently asking each of them to say Masses and prayers for him with diligence; this they gladly promised. But they were all very sad and they all wept, especially because he had said that they would not see his face much longer in this world.

But they rejoiced about one thing he had said: 'It is time, if it so please my Maker, that I should be released from the body and come now to Him who formed me from nothing when I did not exist. I have lived a long time and the Holy Judge has provided well for me during my whole life. The time of my release is near; indeed my soul longs to see Christ my king in all his beauty.' This and many other admirable words he spoke in joy for our great profit until he came to his last day at vesper time.

Then the boy of whom I spoke, Wilbur by name, said again: 'Beloved master, there is still one sentence left, not yet written down.' He answered: 'Write it then.' After a short time the boy said: 'Now it is written.' And he replied: 'Good. It is finished. You have spoken the truth. Take my head in your hands, for it pleases me very much to sit opposite my holy place where I used to pray, so that as I sit there I may call upon my Father.'

And thus, on the floor of his cell singing: 'Glory be to the Father and to the Son and to the Holy Spirit' and the rest, he breathed out his spirit from his body. And it should be believed without doubt that, because he had always worked hard in the praise of God, his soul was carried by angels to the joy of Heaven which he desired. All who heard or saw the death of our blessed father Bede said that they had never seen anyone else end his days with such great devotion and peace. For as you have heard, as long as his soul remained in his body he sang: 'Glory be to the Father' and other words to the glory of God and with hands outstretched did not cease to give thanks to God.

I would like you to know also that much more could be spoken or written about him, but now my ignorant tongue cuts short my words. Nevertheless I intend with God's help to write more fully later what I myself have seen and heard about him.

Here ends the letter of Cuthbert on the death of the venerable Bede, the priest.

Sources

St Aidan and St Oswald

The earliest account of these saints is by Bede in his *Historia Ecclesiastica Gentis Anglorum*. A later Life of St Oswald, written by Aelfric, a monk, around 990– 1002, was based on Bede's account. The text here is from Bede's *Historia Ecclesiastica,* translated by John Gregory in *The Illustrated Bede,* Floris Books, Edinburgh 1996 (London 1989).

St Cuthbert

Bede himself also wrote two lives of St Cuthbert, but the earliest life of the saint was written by an unnamed monk of Lindisfarne, somewhere between 699 and 705, within twenty years of Cuthbert's death. This *Vita Sancti Cuthberti* was written in Latin. The text here is from Bertram Colgrave's *Two Lives of St Cuthbert,* Cambridge 1940, by permission of Cambridge University Press.

The Synod of Whitby

The first account here is from Bede's *Historia Ecclesiastica.* The second is by Eddius Stephanus, translated by Colgrave in *Life of Bishop Wilfrid by Eddius Stephanus,* Cambridge 1927, by permission of Cambridge University Press.

St Wilfrid

Extracts from Eddius Stephanus' Life. Eddius (Aedde) knew Wilfrid well and accompanied him on many of his travels. The Life was written a few years after St Wilfrid's death in 709.

St Hilda

The account here is from Bede's *Historia Ecclesiastica*.

St Bede

The first text is Bede's own autobiographical note in Book V of the *Historia Ecclesiastica*. The second ('The Death of St Bede') is a letter from a monk Cuthbert who later became Abbot of Jarrow, written to Lul soon after 735. The translation is by D.H. Farmer, published in 1990, by permission of Penguin Books, Harmondsworth.